BARK

BARK

A Field Guide to Trees of the Northeast

Michael Wojtech

UNIVERSITY PRESS OF NEW ENGLAND

HANOVER AND LONDON

University Press of New England

www.upne.com

© 2011 University Press of New England

All rights reserved

Manufactured in China

Designed by April Leidig-Higgins

Typeset in The Serif and Zapatista by

Copperline Book Services, Inc.

Library of Congress Cataloging-in-Publication Data
Wojtech, Michael.
Bark : a field guide to trees of the northeast /
Michael Wojtech.
    p. cm.
Includes index.
ISBN 978-1-58465-852-8 (pbk. : alk. paper)
1. Trees—Northeastern States—Indentification.
2. Bark—Northeastern States—Identification.
I. Title.
QK117.W65   2011
582.160974—dc22   2010035175

9 8 7

For
Samantha,
Luna,
and Leo

[T]he notion of the infinite variety of detail and the multiplicity of forms is a pleasing one; in complexity are the fringes of beauty, and in variety are generosity and exuberance. — Annie Dillard

Contents

Foreword xi

Preface xiii

1 **How to Use This Field Guide** 1

2 **Bark Structure** 7

3 **Bark Types** 15

4 **Secondary Identification Keys 1–7** 37

5 **Bark Ecology** 61

6 **Species** 87

Acknowledgments 247

Suggested Reading 249

Bibliography 251

Index 257

*See inside front and back covers for the
Primary Indentification Key.*

Foreword

AS A CHILD between the ages of six and twelve, just about all of my free time was spent in what we kids called The Woods. The Woods lay across the road from my home, a 70-acre forested island surrounded by a surging sea of suburban housing. Without any instruction, I learned how to differentiate trees solely by the appearance of their bark. The shaggy-barked trees were found in the skunk cabbage–covered lowlands, the smooth, gray-barked trees in the drier uplands, and the elegant trees with their soaring, straight trunks in between. It wasn't until many years later, in a dendrology course at the University of New Hampshire, that I learned that these trees had names: red maple, American beech, and tulip tree, respectively.

Ever since that dendrology course, I've wondered why leaf and twig characteristics are the major focus for tree identification. As a young child out in The Woods, I was oblivious to leaves and twigs, but the bark and trunks of trees were always right in front of me. Given that New England broadleaf trees are leafless for more than half the year and critical identification features such as buds often can't be seen from the ground, why the emphasis on leaves and twigs? And even more perplexing, why was there no field guide for identifying trees by bark? The answers to those questions grew clearer when Michael Wojtech asked me to serve as his thesis committee chair in 2003.

At that time Michael was a student in our Conservation Biology Program at Antioch University New England. As we discussed his idea of creating a field guide to regional trees, we both began to see why identifying trees by bark might prove to be a complicated project. In this regard black birch offers an illuminating example.

The bark of black birch goes through four distinct transformations as the tree matures from a sapling to an old-growth monarch. The tree starts out with smooth, black bark etched with horizontal, white lenticels. After about 50 years, the smooth bark starts to crack open, creating vertical fissures. By 100 years of age, these fissures develop into large rectangular plates that curl away from the trunk. At 150 years, most of the rectangular plates are shed, leaving the tree once again with smooth bark—this time lacking lenticels. When a black birch is two centuries old, the bark develops vertical ridges, making it look like some sort of exotic oak.

Michael and I wondered how any guide could incorporate all of these changes in bark characteristics, not only for black birch, but for dozens of other trees. Not to mention the fact that, with some species, even the bark of similar-aged trees can look very different. In my woodlot in Westminster, Vermont, I have a number of 100-year-old red maples. Some of these trees have coarse, shaggy bark reminiscent of a shagbark hickory, while others aren't at all shaggy.

Michael had ventured into a task far more complex than either of us had originally anticipated. However, two of his hallmarks are patience and perseverance. I can't recall the precise number of iterations that the keys to this field guide underwent, but I don't doubt that it was close to a dozen, with Michael ironing out the wrinkles we had uncovered each time.

Through all of this hard work, Michael has created a useful reference that I am confident will garner a large following. His book occupies a niche unto itself. Besides helping people to identify trees while walking though the forest, this guide also reveals the unique tales that tree barks have to tell—stories that explain why the bark of paper birch has evolved to peel or why the black cherry covers its trunk in thousands of scales. One of my personal favorites relates to the rain-soaked trunks of the American beech: they serve as pastures for algae-grazing slugs.

The bark of trees has been relegated to the background for too long. With this guide, Michael Wojtech has prepared a forested pageant for our eyes. I encourage anyone who picks up this book to become acquainted with our sylvan neighbors, as I did more than 50 years ago, by the wonderful ways in which they cloak their strong frames.

Tom Wessels
Professor of Ecology, Antioch University New England

Preface

Perhaps the most radical thing we can do is to stay at home, so we can learn the names of the plants and animals around us; so that we can begin to know what tradition we're part of.
—Terry Tempest Williams

EVERYWHERE I GO I meet people who want to know more about trees. Some, such as those I studied with while earning my Master's degree in Conservation Biology at Antioch University New England, have professional motivations—to determine vital habitats for endangered plants or animals, to prioritize landscapes for preservation, to teach tree identification skills to others. As environmental professionals, we look at individual elements in a landscape and see how they connect together.

I have also listened to others—dancers, teachers, carpenters, businesspeople, parents—about their desire to become familiar with the trees in their local forests. What I feel from everyone, professional or not, is an overriding, foundational desire to make connections with the land where they live, work, or play, be it a wild preserve or a wooded urban lot. A forest as a monochromatic green landscape in summer or a blur of browns and grays in winter can seem remote, distant. Relating to the individual pieces of the forest is an intimate act that can bring us closer to the connection we long for. Beyond the practical, we hope to see the trees through the forest.

When I moved to New England to attend school it was difficult to live in a new town where I didn't know anyone. But it was even more unsettling to find the local forests so unfamiliar. I had left behind the pine barrens of New Jersey, and found myself surrounded by new tree species. I made my first intimate friends here not with the neighbors on my street, but with the trees in a local conservation area as I learned their names—a shaggy yellow birch (*Betula alleghaniensis*) with broad, stout branches that once spread out over a pasture; the young American elms (*Ulmus americana)* growing on the slope adjacent to a wetland; the eastern hemlocks (*Tsuga canadensis),* with cathedral-like open space and a carpet of orange needles below their branches. As Mitchell Thomashow writes in *Bringing the Biosphere Home*: "I find solace in the stability of my home landscape, believing that with increased awareness of the flora and fauna of this place, I will no longer be a transient, one who just passes through. Via intimacy with the local ecology, I aspire to become native."

I have spent countless hours—wandering through forests observing trees, scouring a shelf full of books and journal articles, even leaning out my car window—looking for some nuance of bark that might improve my ability to describe it to others. As tree species have adapted over time to different environmental conditions such as fire, moisture levels, disease, and the influence of animals, their barks have developed a wide variety of textures, shapes, and colors that can be challenging to interpret. Many sources state that identifying trees by their bark requires the "experience" of botanists, foresters, and others who spend much time in the woods. With this book, naturalists at all levels of experience can learn the bark characteristics of trees in the Northeast.

As you focus on bark—and improve your ability to see—I hope that other, equally intimate layers of the forest also become apparent. You may notice the woodpecker mining for ants on a tree trunk; see fox scat on a nearby rock; spot the flowers of an early spring hepatica, almost hidden among last year's leaves. There are always new discoveries to be made. I had been searching for a good specimen of young black cherry (*Prunus serotina*) to photograph for quite some time when I found a suitable tree along the dirt road that I live on—a tree I had walked past hundreds of times without noticing. The art of seeing, and the connection to place, grows exponentially when you learn to stop and observe.

If you want to experience a forest, mingle among its trees. If you want to know the trees, learn their bark.

BARK

1   How to Use This Field Guide

WHEN I GET a new field guide, I'm often so excited that I head straight outdoors without pausing to review the instructions and background information in the book. Inevitably I find myself standing perplexed over an unfamiliar plant or animal sign, not completely sure of how the identification key works or confused about the terminology used. Sometimes I get lucky by randomly flipping through pages, looking for a picture that matches what I see. But more often my growing frustration diminishes some of the enthusiasm and wonder with which I started out. I'm tempted to leave the book behind on subsequent field trips, unsure of its usefulness. But once I review the introductory material and learn how the field guide works, I'm ready to head out and put the book to use.

Whether you are just beginning to learn about trees or are an experienced observer, I encourage you to review the following instructions, along with chapter 2 (bark structure) and chapter 3 (bark types). These sections, while relatively brief, establish foundational criteria for differentiating bark characteristics. You don't need to memorize them; even a basic understanding will make this field guide easier and more enjoyable to use.

Geographic Coverage

This book includes species that grow in New England and eastern
New York State.

Species Covered

The descriptions in this book refer to native or widely naturalized
tree species that grow taller than 30 feet. (You can visualize 30 feet
by imagining the peak of a two-story house.) Identifying trees is
a process of elimination; by excluding shrubs, saplings, and the
youngest specimens of trees—all of which can often be identified
by their more visible leaves, twigs, and buds—the focus of this
guide has been narrowed to a manageable sixty-seven species.
Be cautious when identifying trees in parks and neighborhoods.
Many non-native species that do not appear in these pages are
planted in such areas. Also, make sure the tree you are puzzling
over is still alive. (This may be difficult to determine once the
leaves are down.) The bark on dead trees changes rapidly and is
not easy to classify.

Bark Phases and Descriptions

Some species retain the same bark characteristics for their entire
lifespan. For most species, though, bark appearance changes with
age. For this guide these different bark characteristics have been

consolidated into three phases, beginning when a tree reaches 30 feet in height: young (Y), mature (M), and old (O). While age and bark characteristics are correlated, not enough information is available to designate specific ages for each phase. The onset of each phase does not always relate to size, since growth rates vary according to soil type, light availability, moisture levels, predation, and other factors.

Bark on the upper trunk is younger, and often different in appearance, than that on the lower trunk. Descriptions (unless otherwise noted) refer to the bark at eye level. Since bark characteristics on individual trees can vary, descriptions refer to those traits appearing over more than half the trunk. Photos throughout the book use a quarter, which is approximately 1 inch in diameter, as a size reference.

Five Steps to Identifying Trees by Their Bark

1. Read the introductory chapters.
   > Bark Structure (chapter 2) explains the different bark layers and how they form.
   > Bark Types (chapter 3) uses more detailed descriptions of bark structure to characterize six bark types, which are the basis for the identification keys.
2. Use the Primary Identification Key (inside front cover) to determine the bark type.
   > Start at the beginning, then move sequentially through the key.
   > Find the first bark type that matches the tree you are identifying. (Some species match multiple types, but they are only included in one key.)
3. Turn to the corresponding Secondary Key (1–7) in chapter 4, as indicated.
   > Steps in the keys are numbered; start at the beginning, then follow sequentially until you find a match.
4. Use the detailed descriptions and supplementary information in the Species pages (the page number is noted in the key) to confirm your findings, to narrow your choices if you are unsure about a particular specimen, or to differentiate among species that have such similar bark that they are listed together in the key.

5. Most importantly, have fun. Make a game out it. When approaching an unfamiliar tree keep your focus glued to the trunk—don't allow yourself to look at other characteristics of the tree or the surroundings until you've tried to identify it. Even if you are perplexed, try working through the Primary Key to determine the bark type. With practice you will learn to notice smaller and smaller details about bark, until one day you realize that recognizing bark characteristics has become second nature.

Bark Ecology

Chapter 5 moves away from species identification to explore some of the reasons why such a variety of bark characteristics have evolved. It also describes human uses of bark and other interspecies adaptations associated with bark.

Species

Chapter 6 provides detailed information for each of the sixty-seven species included in the book.

NAMES

Species are arranged by family, then listed alphabetically by scientific name. The white oak and red oak groups are additionally divided. Taxonomy used throughout the book comes from Gleason and Cronquist's *Manual of Vascular Plants of Northeastern United States and Adjacent Canada*. Each entry begins with the species' common name(s), followed by the scientific name, then the family. For example, the entry for sugar maple begins like this:

> **sugar maple** (hard maple, rock maple)
> *Acer saccharum* Marshall
> maple family—Aceraceae

The scientific name typically consists of three parts: the genus (*Acer*), which groups closely related species together; the species (*saccharum*); and the person that described or identified the species (in this case, Humphrey Marshall). Using the scientific name ensures the proper identification of a tree, since most species have more than one common name and these names sometimes overlap. Both *Carpinus caroliniana* and *Ostrya virginiana*, for example, are referred to as ironwood. The best-known common name is listed first. Both scientific and common names appear in the index.

DESCRIPTIONS AND PHOTOS

The bark of young, mature, and old specimens, along with special bark characteristics (where applicable), are depicted for each species. These descriptions and photos include the most common bark characteristics for each species, but they do not completely represent the variation that exists in nature.

HABITAT

This section briefly describes the environment in which a species naturally grows. Don't forget, however, that trees are often planted in parks and occasionally grow in other areas outside of their natural habitat.

NOTES

This section contains supplemental information such as bark ecology, comparisons with similar species, and descriptions of human uses.

BRANCH-AND-LEAF PATTERN

This classification applies only to hardwood species; it is not relevant for conifers. Of the species included in this guide, only members of the maple (Aceraceae) and ash (Oleaceae) families have opposite branch-and-leaf patterns; all others are alternate. Branch-and-leaf patterns are represented by the following icons.

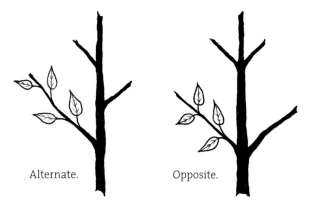

Alternate.   Opposite.

LEAVES

Even within a single species, leaves are produced in a variety of shapes and sizes. Illustrations of the most common forms for each species, with references to average size, are provided to help confirm your bark diagnosis.

RANGE MAPS

The ranges shown in this book describe the regions in which a species maintains a consistent population. Scattered specimens can sometimes be found outside these regions, depending on localized climate and soil conditions. The data set for the range maps, produced by the U.S. Geological Survey, represents species ranges presented in book form by Elbert Little.

2 Bark Structure

IN THE EARLY STAGES this project, I photographed the different phases of bark for all sixty-seven tree species in this book. With these photos spread across my office floor, I spent months staring at a blur of textured browns and grays, trying to group them by similarities. During the same period, I studied botany texts and other writings about bark. Over time I realized that these stacks of photos—such as those showing smooth, unbroken bark or those depicting deep furrows and thick ridges—neatly corresponded to the ways in which bark layers form and then grow. This principle provides the foundational criteria used throughout this book to identify trees by their bark.

A basic understanding of bark structure will help you see past the browns and grays, to notice the details that identify the bark of each species. Individual bark layers, italicized at first mention in the text, are described in the order in which they develop on a growing tree and are listed in table 2.1.

Envision the cross section of a tree trunk—perhaps the stump of a tree that has recently been cut down. The band of bark around the circumference can be easily differentiated from the wood to the inside of it. The term *bark* refers to all of the layers in the outer shell of a tree that can be detached from the wood. That is, everything outside a thin ring of tissue called the *vascular cambium* (fig. 2.1). In spring, when growth is most active, the vascular cambium appears as a slimy layer that remains on the wood when the bark is removed.

Most growth in the diameter of the trunk and branches is a result of cell division that takes place in the vascular cambium. Each

2.1 LAYERS AND DESCRIPTIONS

Layer	Description
active phloem	Conductive tissue in the inner bark that transports the products of photosynthesis vertically and horizontally throughout the tree.
cork (phellem)	Outer, protective layer of the periderm, consisting of cells that die as they mature.
cork cambium (phellogen)	Middle layer of the periderm; a secondary layer of cell division and growth that forms cork skin to the inside and cork to the outside.
cork skin (phelloderm)	Thin inner layer of the periderm (present in most but not all species) that contains chlorophyll and is capable of photosynthesis.
inner bark	The living portion of bark, consisting of the active phloem and the cork skin and cork cambium of the active periderm.
lenticels	Small pores through the protective outer bark that allow gas exchange between the living tissues of the inner bark and the surrounding air.
outer bark	Non-living portion of the bark, consisting of the cork layer of the active periderm and, for most species, the rhytidome.
periderm	Protective layer consisting of cork skin (in most but not all species), cork cambium, and cork. Bark can consist of one periderm or a series of periderms.
—active periderm	The most recently created periderm, which forms within the active phloem to the inside of the previously formed periderm.
—initial periderm	The first periderm, formed in a continuous layer around the circumference.
rhytidome	Alternating layers of old periderms and dead phloem tissue. Provides protection, often thickens over time. Trees with a persistent initial periderm do not have a rhytidome.
vascular cambium	The main location of cell division and growth in thickness of the tree. It forms wood to the inside and inner bark (active phloem) to the outside.

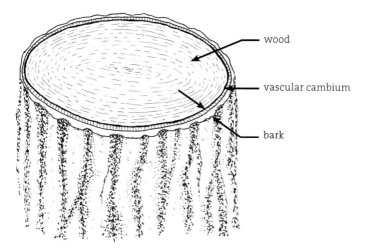

wood

vascular cambium

bark

Fig. 2.1. Cross section of a tree trunk.

season the vascular cambium forms a ring of wood to its inside. To the outside, the vascular cambium produces a thinner layer of bark tissue called the *active phloem*, though not in annual increments that can be counted.

Cells produced by the vascular cambium (fig. 2.2) make up the circulatory system of a tree. The new layers of wood distribute water and nutrients upward from the roots to the leaves. New layers of active phloem in the bark transport sugars and nutrients —the products of photosynthesis—throughout the tree. Specialized cells in the active phloem—especially fiber cells—affect bark appearance, and they often hold waste products of metabolism, such as resins and tannins.

Outside the active phloem, a layer called the *periderm* protects the circulatory system of the tree from environmental elements like heat, cold, insects, and desiccation. The periderm usually consists of three layers (fig. 2.2). The middle layer, the *cork cambium*, is an area of cell division and growth that produces *cork skin* to the inside and *cork* to the outside. Cork skin, present in most but not all tree species, can be as thin as a single layer of cells. It often contains chlorophyll and is capable of photosynthesis. In most cases you can reveal the green cork skin by scraping a twig with your fingernail.

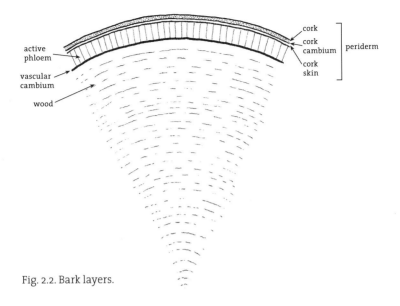

active phloem

vascular cambium

wood

cork

cork cambium } periderm

cork skin

Fig. 2.2. Bark layers.

To the outside, the cork cambium produces cork, which prevents the trunk and branches from drying out and protects against fungal and bacterial infection. Many thin layers of cork can be produced each year. The cork cells die as they mature, but they retain their protective qualities. The dead, empty cells also help insulate the tree and account for the light weight of bark.

As wood thickens, it pushes out against the slower-growing bark that surrounds it. The way bark adapts to this pressure differs in each species. Does the bark expand to accommodate the growth of wood, or do outer layers eventually split apart? What shapes do outer layers form as they break apart? Do older layers of bark stay adhered to the trunk, or do they fall off? The answers to these questions, which depend on how the layers of bark form, provide the basis for identifying tree species by their bark.

The smooth, unbroken outer surface on young trunks and branches is the cork layer of the *initial periderm*. This periderm forms a continuous protective layer around the tree. A small number of tree species in the Northeast, such as American beech (*Fagus grandifolia*), have a single persistent periderm for their entire lifespan. In these species, the periderm expands to match the growth of the wood beneath it and remains unbroken (fig. 2.3).

Fig. 2.3. Initials carved 27 years ago in the bark of an American beech show how bark expands as the trunk grows in diameter.

The bark characteristics of most species, however, change with age. The periderm must expand 3 inches around the circumference of the trunk and branches for every 1 inch of wood that is added beneath it. Over time, if the initial periderm can't stretch or grow quickly enough, it splits and breaks apart—like a too-tight pair of jeans. The initial periderm on some species, such as shagbark hickory (*Carya ovata*), can break apart after only a few years (fig. 2.4). Others remain smooth for a longer time; the trunks of silver maple (*Acer saccharinum*) can reach 1 foot in diameter before cracks appear (fig. 2.5).

An intact periderm layer, however, provides essential protection from outside elements. When the initial periderm begins to break apart, a new layer—called the *active periderm*—forms to the inside of the older one, within the active phloem tissue. This new periderm can form in one piece around the trunk's circumference or in overlapping sections that vary in size and shape according to species. Any cells trapped outside the active periderm—both phloem tissue and the old periderm layers—become isolated and

Fig. 2.4. (*Left*) The initial periderm layer, broken and split, on a young shagbark hickory.

Fig. 2.5. (*Right*) Cracks in the initial periderm layer of a large silver maple.

die. This process can repeat itself continually as the tree grows. The alternating layers of old periderm and dead phloem tissue form a protective layer called the *rhytidome*, named after the Greek word for wrinkle (fig. 2.6).

Although trees need the protection of the non-living cork and rhytidome, they also need a controlled way to exchange gases between the inner, living tissues beneath these layers and the surrounding air. This function is accomplished by small pores called *lenticels* (fig. 2.7). These structures, which occur in a variety of shapes and sizes, are often visible on smooth bark but can be difficult to see in the cracks and furrows of rough, thicker bark.

Bark, then, consists of the living cells in the *inner bark*—the active phloem, the cork skin, and the cork cambium—and the dead

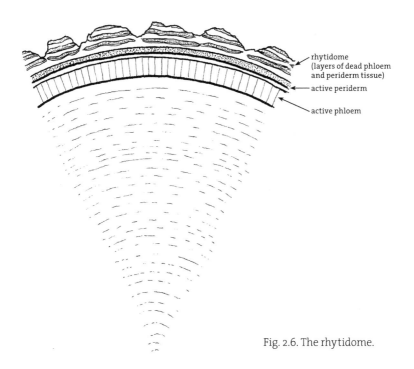

rhytidome
(layers of dead phloem
and periderm tissue)

active periderm

active phloem

Fig. 2.6. The rhytidome.

Fig. 2.7. Buff-colored, dash-like lenticels on the trunk of a young northern red oak (*Quercus rubra*).

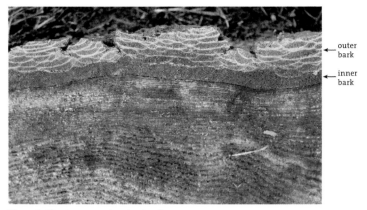

outer bark

inner bark

Fig. 2.8. The inner and outer bark.

cells that make up the *outer bark*—the cork layer of the active periderm and, on most trees, the rhytidome (fig. 2.8). The thickness of bark varies according to species—about 0.25 inch for an American beech 1 foot in diameter, for example, but over 1-inch thick on some oaks of similar size.

The outer bark's variety of textures, shapes, and thicknesses reflect its reaction to the stress caused by the expanding wood beneath it. The bark of each species responds differently, depending on the number of periderms (one or multiple), the type of periderm (continuous or in overlapping sections), and the type of phloem tissue (especially the amount and type of fiber cells)—just as what happens to an over-tight pair of jeans depends on the material from which it is made and how that material is woven together.

3 Bark Types

THE STRUCTURE OF bark provides criteria for defining six distinct types: smooth, unbroken; peeling horizontally in curly strips; visible lenticels; vertical cracks or seams in otherwise smooth bark; scales, plates and vertical strips; and ridges and furrows. A familiarity with these descriptions is necessary for using the Primary Identification Key, as well as the Secondary Keys.

The bark of some species, such as American beech (*Fagus grandifolia*), retains the same characteristics as the tree ages. Most species, however, show dramatic changes, which means that an individual species may correspond to more than one bark type. This guide categorizes up to three phases of bark characteristics for each species: young (Y), mature (M), and old (O). Young northern red oak (*Quercus rubra*) starts with smooth, unbroken bark, for example, but its mature bark features thick ridges broken by furrows (fig. 3.1).

Some species also may correspond to more than one bark type at a given growth phase. Mature paper birch (*Betula papyrifera*) has bark that peels horizontally in curly strips; its bark also has visible lenticels (fig. 3.2). To complicate matters slightly more, two similarly sized trees of the same species can have markedly different bark types (fig. 3.3). A tree's age is a more accurate predictor of bark characteristics than its size.

The following illustrations and photographs show typical examples of the variation within each bark type.

Fig. 3.1. Unbroken bark of a young northern red oak (left) compared with the thick ridges and furrows on a mature specimen (right).

Fig. 3.2. Bark of a mature paper birch.

Fig. 3.3. Compare a young silver maple (left), with vertical cracks in otherwise smooth bark, and a mature specimen of the same species (below), only slightly larger in diameter, with thick, multi-layered bark broken into vertical strips.

Smooth, Unbroken

Bark of this type is not peeling, cracked, or furrowed. Smooth, unbroken bark is found on many young trees, and some species retain this bark type as they grow older. The visible surface is the cork layer of the initial periderm, which comprises the entire outer bark (fig. 3.4). Once mature, this cork layer typically maintains a constant thickness; in each growing season, new cork cells are created while old cells die. The dead cells slough off imperceptibly, or show as a powdery substance on the outer surface, as on young quaking aspen (*Populus tremuloides*) and gray birch (*Betula populifolia*). Figures 3.5 and 3.6 show two examples of smooth, unbroken bark.

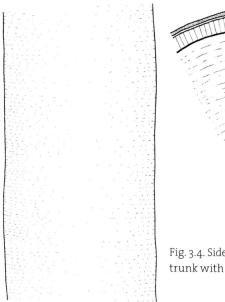

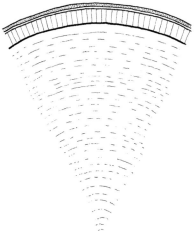

Fig. 3.4. Side view and cross section of trunk with smooth, unbroken bark.

Fig. 3.5. Mature
American beech
(*Fagus grandifolia*).

Fig. 3.6. Mature
American hornbeam
(*Carpinus caroliniana*).

Peeling Horizontally in Curly Strips

As in trees with smooth bark, the visible surface of trees that peel horizontally in curly strips is the cork layer of the initial periderm. On these species, stress from the expansion of wood beneath the bark causes the thin, papery, outermost layer of cork—often only a few cells thick—to peel away from the trunk (fig. 3.7). On some species this peeling mechanism keeps the cork layer at a constant thickness. Figures 3.8 and 3.9 show examples of bark peeling horizontally in curly strips.

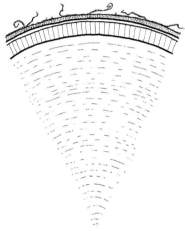

Fig. 3.7. Side view and cross section of trunk with bark peeling horizontally in curly strips.

Fig. 3.8. Young river birch (*Betula nigra*).

Fig. 3.9. Mature yellow birch (*Betula alleghaniensis*).

Visible Lenticels

Almost all trees have lenticels—small pores that allow gas exchange through the protective layers of the outer bark. On smooth bark, lenticels can be easy to see and useful for species identification. On most species, however, lenticels become hidden in cracks or furrows as the bark thickens.

Lenticels can be linear, diamond-shaped, oval, or round (fig. 3.10), and are often a different color from the surrounding bark. As a tree grows and the periderm expands, lenticels can stretch horizontally, in the same way that initials carved into a beech tree's smooth bark can expand. Other species have single lenticels that break into smaller sections as the tree grows, while lenticels on some species remain the same size. Outer layers of bark that peel or flake off uncover new lenticels in the layers below them. Figures 3.11, 3.12, and 3.13 show examples of bark with visible lenticels.

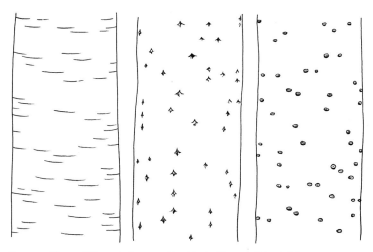

Fig. 3.10. Three different shapes of lenticels (*from left to right*): linear, diamond-shaped, oval or round.

Fig. 3.11. (*Above*) Linear lenticels on young paper birch (*Betula papyrifera*).

Fig. 3.12. (*Right, top*) Diamond-shaped lenticels on young bigtooth aspen (*Populus grandidentata*).

Fig. 3.13. (*Right, bottom*) Round or oval lenticels on young pin oak (*Quercus palustris*).

Vertical Cracks or Seams in Otherwise Smooth Bark

When the smooth, initial periderm is no longer able to accommodate a tree's growth, it can break apart in a number of different ways. The bark of many species develops vertical seams or cracks (fig. 3.14). Seams are like stretch marks; they appear in areas where the initial periderm is stressed but has not yet split. Cracks often begin at lenticels, which are the weakest part of the periderm. Both cracks and seams expose layers of phloem tissue that have died and become part of the outer bark. Sometimes the color of this phloem tissue is useful for species identification; in young hickory trees, for example, cracks and seams often reveal an orange color. Figures 3.15 and 3.16 show examples of cracks or seams in otherwise smooth bark.

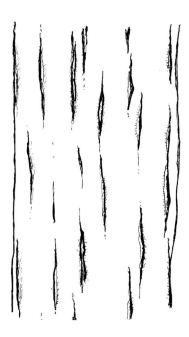

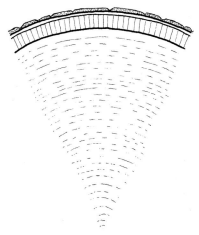

Fig. 3.14. Side view and cross section of trunk with vertical cracks or seams in otherwise smooth bark.

Fig. 3.15. Young pignut
hickory (*Carya glabra*).

Fig. 3.16. Young scarlet
oak (*Quercus coccinea*).

Scales, Plates, and Vertical Strips

As new layers of wood press outward on the bark, layers of the rhytidome can break apart into scales, plates, or vertical strips. These features can vary in shape and size according to species and age. Their thickness also varies, ranging from paper-thin and flexible to thick and stiff. The characteristics of the periderm and the phloem tissue of each species determine the thickness of the rhytidome, what shapes it breaks into, and how the layers adhere to each other. Some species have scales, plates, or vertical strips that fall off after a new layer has formed beneath them. On other species multiple layers build in thickness.

For all species in this category, the exterior layer or layers of the outer bark—scales, plates, or vertical strips—appear as if they could be pried away from the rest of the bark, and they often separate from the trunk on one or more sides. By contrast, even the outermost layer on trees that have bark with furrows and ridges (described in the next section) appear rigid and fixed.

SCALES

Bark with scales has rhytidome layers that break apart along the borders of small, overlapping sections of periderm (fig. 3.17). On a single tree, the scales are roughly similar in size, though their individual shapes can vary. Figures 3.18 and 3.19 show examples of bark with scales.

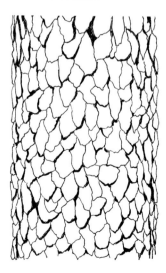
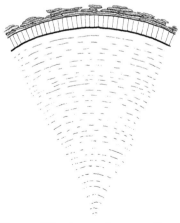

Fig. 3.17. Side view and cross section of trunk with scales.

Fig. 3.18. Mature black cherry
(*Prunus serotina*).

Fig. 3.19. Young red spruce
(*Picea rubens*).

PLATES

Plated bark forms when groups of small, overlapping sections of periderm are held together by fibrous tissue, or where new periderms form in large, variably shaped sections (fig. 3.20). Plates are larger and typically thicker and stiffer than scales, with the exception in this region being the thin, somewhat pliable plates of sycamore (*Platanus occidentalis*). Figures 3.21 and 3.22 show examples of bark with plates.

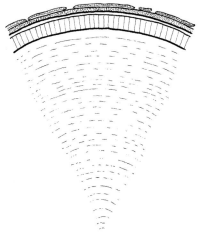

Fig. 3.20. Side view and cross section of trunk with plates.

Fig. 3.22. Mature black birch (*Betula lenta*).

Fig. 3.21. Young sycamore (*Platanus occidentalis*).

VERTICAL STRIPS

Vertical strips are at least three times longer than wide. Periderms typically form in long, vertically oriented sections due to the way that interlocking fibrous tissue bands together. Rhytidome layers can break apart along the boundaries of these sections to form vertical strips (fig. 3.23). A few species in this category, such as northern white cedar (*Thuja occidentalis*), have periderms that form a continuous ring around the tree. As wood beneath the bark grows and exerts pressure, the outer layers of the rhytidome split into vertical strips. These species are often shaggy in appearance. Figures 3.24 and 3.25 show examples of bark with vertical strips.

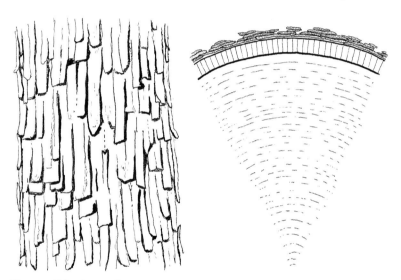

Fig. 3.23. Side view and cross section of trunk with vertical strips.

Fig. 3.24. Mature northern
white cedar (*Thuja occidentalis*).

Fig. 3.25. Mature red maple (*Acer rubrum*).

Ridges and Furrows

Like trees with scales, plates, or vertical strips, trees with furrowed and ridged bark also have periderms that form in sections. In these trees, groups of periderm sections are held together by fibrous tissue. Bands of fiber cells also keep multiple layers of rhytidome closely adhered to each other. As these layers build in thickness, they form vertical ridges separated by increasingly deep furrows (fig. 3.26). Individual layers—even the outer ones—are not easy to separate from each other, and outer layers are shed in small, often unnoticeable quantities.

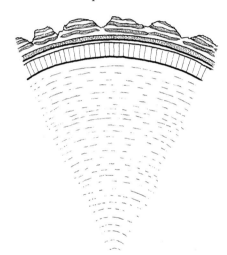

Fig. 3.26. Cross section of trunk with ridges and furrows.

There are three general forms of furrowed and ridged bark: ridges that intersect, ridges broken horizontally, and uninterrupted ridges. A single species can exhibit one or a combination of these forms, depending on the type and quantity of fibrous tissue present.

INTERSECTING RIDGES

As a tree expands in diameter, fibrous tissue that runs around the trunk's circumference can prevent ridges from completely separating from each other, creating ridges that intersect (fig. 3.27). The furrows formed by intersecting ridges can have a variety of sizes and shapes. Species with a large amount of such fiber have small, diamond-shaped furrows, while those species with less fiber have mostly parallel ridges that occasionally intersect. Figures 3.28 and 3.29 show examples of bark with intersecting ridges.

Fig. 3.27. Trunk with intersecting ridges.

Fig. 3.28. Mature white ash (*Fraxinus americana*).

Fig. 3.29. Mature sassafras (*Sassafras albidum*).

Species with lesser amounts of vertically oriented fibrous tissue have ridges that are broken horizontally (fig. 3.30). Cracks can occur in the outer layer of the rhytidome or through multiple layers, breaking the ridges into consistently or irregularly shaped segments. The ridges may also intersect. Figures 3.31 and 3.32 show examples of bark with ridges broken horizontally.

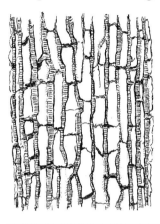

Fig. 3.30. Trunk with ridges that are broken horizontally.

Fig. 3.31. Mature black oak (*Quercus velutina*).

Fig. 3.32. Mature eastern cottonwood (*Populus deltoides*).

UNINTERRUPTED RIDGES

Bark in this category has ridges that are not interrupted for 12-inch or longer segments (fig. 3.33). Vertically oriented fibers keep the ridges from being broken horizontally with any regularity. Because the fibrous tissue that runs around the circumference is relatively weak, ridges separate cleanly and do not regularly intersect. The bark of older specimens, however, may begin to intersect or to break horizontally, especially at the base. Figures 3.34 and 3.35 show examples of bark with uninterrupted ridges.

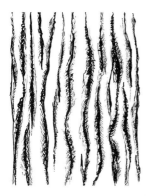

Fig. 3.33. Trunk with uninterrupted ridges.

Fig. 3.34. Young tulip tree (*Liriodendron tulipifera*).

Fig. 3.35. Mature northern red oak (*Quercus rubra*).

4 Secondary Identification Keys 1–7

How to Use This Key

For best results, review How to Use This Field Guide (chapter 1), Bark Structure (chapter 2) and Bark Types (chapter 3) before using these identification keys.

A. Use the Primary Key on the inside front cover to determine which key (1–7) you should use.
B. Find the *first* bark type that matches the tree you are identifying. [Some species match more than one type. For example, mature paper birch (*Betula papyrifera*) has bark that peels horizontally in curly strips and is included in key 1. This species also has visible lenticels, but it is not included in key 2.]
C. Start at the beginning and move sequentially through the key.
D. Each species listed in the key carries a prefix of Y (young), M (mature), or O (old).
E. The page number that follows each species name directs you to descriptions and photographs on the corresponding Species pages.
F. The details listed on the Species pages can be used to narrow your choices if you are unsure about a particular specimen, or to differentiate between species that have such similar bark that they are listed together in the key.

KEY 1
Peeling Horizontally in Curly Strips

1	Lenticels are clearly visible. → Go to 2.	
	Lenticels are not clearly visible. → Y river birch (*Betula nigra*) 110	
2	Bark is bronze to yellow. → M yellow birch (*Betula alleghaniensis*) 106	
	Bark is not bronze to yellow. → Go to 3.	
3	Peeling layer is white. → M paper birch (*Betula papyrifera*) 112	
	Peeling layer is not white. → M pin cherry (*Prunus pensylvanica*) 214	

Y = young | M = mature | O = old

KEY 2
Lenticels Visible

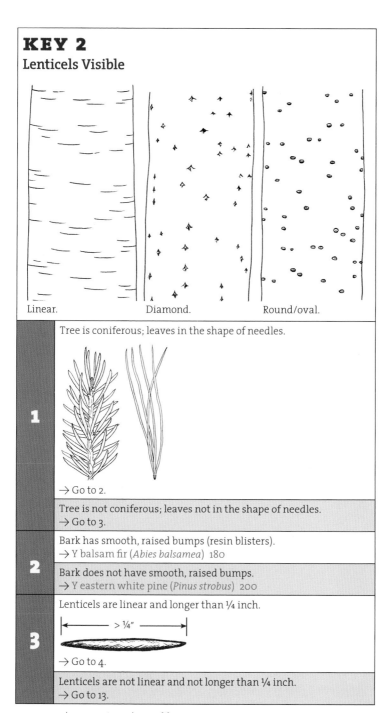

Linear.   Diamond.   Round/oval.

1

Tree is coniferous; leaves in the shape of needles.

→ Go to 2.

Tree is not coniferous; leaves not in the shape of needles.
→ Go to 3.

2

Bark has smooth, raised bumps (resin blisters).
→ Y balsam fir (*Abies balsamea*) 180

Bark does not have smooth, raised bumps.
→ Y eastern white pine (*Pinus strobus*) 200

3

Lenticels are linear and longer than ¼ inch.

|← — > ¼″ — →|

→ Go to 4.

Lenticels are not linear and not longer than ¼ inch.
→ Go to 13.

Y = young | M = mature | O = old

4	Bark is white or whitish. → Go to 5.
	Bark is not white. → Go to 6.
5	Lenticels are black. → Y & M gray birch (*Betula populifolia*) 114
	Lenticels are not black. → Y quaking aspen (*Populus tremuloides*) 230
6	Bark is broken into scales or plates. → Go to 7.
	Bark is not broken into scales or plates. → Go to 9.
7	Lenticels are less than ⅛ inch thick. → Go to 8.
	Lenticels are at least ⅛ inch thick. → O yellow birch (*Betula alleghaniensis*) 106
8	Multiple layers are broken into scales or plates. → M black cherry (*Prunus serotina*) 216
	Only outer layer is cracked or broken into plates. → M black birch (*Betula lenta*) 108
9	Cut or scraped bark (on young trunk, branches and twigs) has wintergreen smell. → Go to 10.
	Cut or scraped bark does not have wintergreen smell. → Go to 11.
10	Bark is dark reddish-brown to gray. → Y black birch (*Betula lenta*) 108
	Bark is bronze to yellowish-gray. → Y yellow birch (*Betula alleghaniensis*) 106
11	Cut or scraped bark (on young trunk, branches, and twigs) has bitter almond smell. → Y black cherry (*Prunus serotina*) 216
	Cut or scraped bark does not have bitter almond smell. → Go to 12.
12	Lenticels are lighter in color than bark. → Y & M American mountain ash (*Sorbus americana*) 218 → Y & M showy mountain ash (*Sorbus decora*) 220
	Lenticels are not lighter in color than bark. → M pin cherry (*Prunus pensylvanica*) 214
13	Lenticels are diamond-shaped. → Go to 14.
	Lenticels are not diamond-shaped. → Go to 16.

Y = young | M = mature | O = old

14	Bark has whitish or blackish vertical lines. → M striped maple (*Acer pensylvanicum*) 90
	Bark has no whitish or blackish vertical lines. → Go to 15.
15	Upper trunk and branches are lighter in color than base. → Y quaking aspen (*Populus tremuloides*) 230 → Y bigtooth aspen (*Populus grandidentata*) 226 → Y balsam poplar (*Populus balsamifera*) 222
	Upper trunk and branches are same color as base. → Y white ash (*Fraxinus americana*) 174
16	Bark is broken into small squarish scales or blocks. → Y box elder (*Acer negundo*) 88
	Bark is not broken into small squarish scales or blocks. → Y pin oak (*Quercus palustris*) 148 → Y northern red oak (*Quercus rubra*) 150 → Y scarlet oak (*Quercus coccinea*) 146

Y = young | M = mature | O = old

KEY 3
Smooth, Unbroken

1	Tree is coniferous; leaves in the shape of needles. → Go to 2.
	Tree is not coniferous; leaves not in the shape of needles. → Go to 3.
2	Bark has smooth, raised bumps (resin blisters) filled with a fragrant resin. → Y & M balsam fir (*Abies balsamea*) 180
	Bark does not have smooth, raised bumps. → Y white spruce (*Picea glauca*) 186
3	Trunk is fluted, sinewy, and muscular-looking. → Y & M American hornbeam (*Carpinus caroliniana*) 116
	Trunk is not fluted, sinewy, and muscular-looking. → Go to 4.

Y = young | M = mature | O = old

4

Bark has vertical lines.

→ Go to 5.

Bark does not have vertical lines.
→ Y & M American beech (*Fagus grandifolia*) 128
→ Y red maple (*Acer rubrum*) 94
→ Y silver maple (*Acer saccharinum*) 98

5

Lines on bark are white or whitish.
→ M striped maple (*Acer pensylvanicum*) 90

Lines on bark are not white or whitish.
→ Go to 6.

6

Lines on bark are orangish.
→ Y bitternut hickory (*Carya cordiformis*) 156
→ Y mockernut hickory (*Carya tomentosa*) 162
→ Y pignut hickory (*Carya glabra*) 158
→ Y shagbark hickory (*Carya ovata*) 160

Lines on bark are not orangish.
→ Go to 7.

7

Bark is light gray.
→ Y downy serviceberry (*Amelanchier arborea*) 212

Bark is not light gray.
→ O striped maple (*Acer pensylvanicum*) 90

Y = young | M = mature | O = old

KEY 4
Vertical Cracks or Seams in Otherwise Smooth Bark

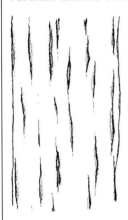

1	Cracks and bark at edges of cracks are blackened. → M downy serviceberry (*Amelanchier arborea*) 212
	Cracks and bark at edges of cracks are not blackened. → Go to 2.
2	Bark between cracks or seams is crowned.  → Y mockernut hickory (*Carya tomentosa*) 162 → Y pignut hickory (*Carya glabra*) 158 → Y shagbark hickory (*Carya ovata*) 160
	Bark between cracks or seams is not crowned. → Go to 3.
3	Cracks or seams are yellow to orange. → Y bitternut hickory (*Carya cordiformis*) 156 → Y Norway maple (*Acer platanoides*) 92
	Cracks or seams are not yellow to orange. → Go to 4.

Y = young | M = mature | O = old

4	Cracks or seams are red or have reddish or pinkish tinge. → Y northern red oak (*Quercus rubra*) 150 → Y pin oak (*Quercus palustris*) 148 → Y scarlet oak (*Quercus coccinea*) 146
	Cracks or seams are not red or do not have reddish or pinkish tinge. → Go to 5.
5	Cracks are all or mostly whitish. → Y tulip tree (*Liriodendron tulipifera*) 170
	Cracks are not all or mostly whitish. → Go to 6.
6	Centers of cracks or entire cracks are rusty-brown to milk-chocolate brown. → Y butternut (*Juglans cinerea*) 164
	Cracks are not rusty-brown to milk-chocolate brown. → Go to 7.
7	Bark has horizontal hairline cracks between vertical cracks. → Y American basswood (*Tilia americana*) 236
	Bark does not have horizontal hairline cracks between vertical cracks. → Go to 8
8	Bark between vertical cracks is crackled, like old paint. → Y sugar maple (*Acer saccharum*) 100
	Bark between vertical cracks is not crackled. → Y red maple (*Acer rubrum*) 94 → Y silver maple (*Acer saccharinum*) 98

Y = young | M = mature | O = old

KEY 5
Vertical Strips

1	Tree is coniferous; leaves in the shape of scales.  → Y & M Atlantic white cedar (*Chamaecyparis thyoides*) 120 → Y & M eastern red cedar (*Juniperus virginiana*) 122 → Y & M northern white cedar (*Thuja occidentalis*) 124
	Tree is not coniferous; leaves not in the shape of scales. → Go to 2.
2	Bark is soft and spongy (can be easily dented with a fingernail). → Go to 3.
	Bark is not soft and spongy. → Go to 4.
3	Cross section of strip (small piece can be easily removed) has alternating light and dark layers. → M American elm (*Ulmus americana*) 240
	Cross section of bark does not have alternating light and dark layers. → Y American elm (*Ulmus americana*) 240 → Y slippery elm (*Ulmus rubra*) 244

Y = young | M = mature | O = old

4	Vertical strips intersect.  → M bitternut hickory (*Carya cordiformis*) 156 → M pignut hickory (*Carya glabra*) 158
	Vertical strips do not intersect. → Go to 5.
5	Strips are papery thin and flexible (thinner than the cover of a paperback book). → Go to 6.
	Strips are thicker and stiffer than the cover of a paperback book. → Go to 9.
6	Strips have straight, parallel sides and squarish ends; similar in width.  → Y hophornbeam (*Ostrya virginiana*) 118
	Strips do not have straight, parallel sides and squarish ends; not similar in width. → Go to 7.
7	Bark on branches peels in ragged, papery sheets. → Y swamp white oak (*Quercus bicolor*) 136
	Bark on branches does not peel in ragged, papery sheets. → Go to 8.

Y = young | M = mature | O = old

8	Bark on branches has corky, wing-like projections. Cross section of branch. → Y bur oak (*Quercus macrocarpa*) 138
	Bark on branches does not have corky, wing-like projections. → Y chinquapin oak (*Quercus muehlenbergii*) 140 → Y post oak (*Quercus stellata*) 144 → Y white oak (*Quercus alba*) 132 → Y black gum (*Nyssa sylvatica*) 172
9	Cracks and edges of vertical strips are blackened. → M downy serviceberry (*Amelanchier arborea*) 212
	Cracks and edges of vertical strips are not blackened. → Go to 10.
10	Strips on lower trunk curl outward on one side. Cross section of trunk. → Go to 11.
	Strips on lower trunk do not curl outward on one side. → Go to 12.
11	Surface of strips is flaky. → M slippery elm (*Ulmus rubra*) 244
	Surface of strips is not flaky. → M sugar maple (*Acer saccharum*) 100

Y = young | M = mature | O = old

12	Strips on upper trunk and branches (not on lower trunk) curl outward on one side. → M white oak (*Quercus alba*) 132
	Strips on upper trunk and branches do not curl outward on one side. → Go to 13.
13	Strips are straight, with parallel sides. → M hophornbeam (*Ostrya virginiana*) 118
	Strips are not straight with parallel sides. → Go to 14.
14	Outer surface of strips is scaly or flaky. → M red maple (*Acer rubrum*) 94 → M silver maple (*Acer saccharinum*) 98 → M willow (*Salix* spp.) 234
	Outer surface of strips is not scaly or flaky. → Go to 15.
15	Strips curl away from trunk on one or both ends. → Y & M shagbark hickory (*Carya ovata*) 160
	Strips do not curl away from trunk on one or both ends. → M chinquapin oak (*Quercus muehlenbergii*) 140

Y = young | M = mature | O = old

KEY 6
Scales or Plates

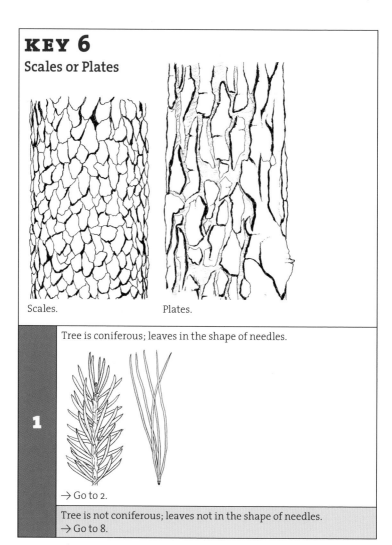

Scales.   Plates.

Tree is coniferous; leaves in the shape of needles.

1

→ Go to 2.

Tree is not coniferous; leaves not in the shape of needles.
→ Go to 8.

Y = young | M = mature | O = old

Bark is shredded into fine, papery scales.

→ Y Norway spruce (*Picea abies*) 184
→ Y red spruce (*Picea rubens*) 190
→ Y black spruce (*Picea mariana*) 188

Bark is not shredded into fine, papery scales.
→ Go to 3.

3

Freshly exposed bark (especially on the underside of scales) is purple.
→ Y & M eastern hemlock (*Tsuga canadensis*) 204

Freshly exposed bark is not purple.
→ Go to 4.

4

Scales have fine, horizontal, evenly spaced cracks (like lines on writing paper).

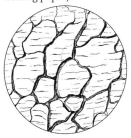

→ Y eastern white pine (*Pinus strobus*) 200

Scales do not have fine, horizontal, evenly spaced cracks.
→ Go to 5.

5

Outer surface of scales is even and contiguous with the circumference of the trunk.

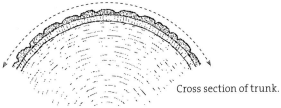

Cross section of trunk.

→ Y & M red pine (*Pinus resinosa*) 194

Outer surface of scales is uneven, not contiguous with the circumference of the trunk.
→ Go to 6.

6	Bark is divided by furrows into blocks with irregular scales smaller than 1 inch. → M eastern white pine (*Pinus strobus*) 200
	Bark is not divided by furrows into blocks with irregular scales smaller than 1 inch. → Go to 7.
7	Scales (or closely pressed layers of scales) curl outward on top and bottom. Longitudinal section of trunk. → Y & M pitch pine (*Pinus rigida*) 196 → M jack pine (*Pinus banksiana*) 192
	Scales do not curl outward on top and bottom. → M black spruce (*Picea mariana*) 188 → Y jack pine (*Pinus banksiana*) 192 → M Norway spruce (*Picea abies*) 184 → M red spruce (*Picea rubens*) 190 → Y & M tamarack (*Larix laricina*) 182 → M white spruce (*Picea glauca*) 186
8	Upper trunk and branches are whitish. → Y & M sycamore (*Platanus occidentalis*) 208
	Upper trunk and branches are not whitish. → Go to 9.
9	Newly exposed scales are red. → Y & M tamarack (*Larix laricina*) 182
	Newly exposed scales are not red. → Go to 10.
10	Bark is soft and spongy. → Y & M black ash (*Fraxinus nigra*) 176 → Y American elm (*Ulmus americana*) 240 → Y slippery elm (*Ulmus rubra*) 244
	Bark is not soft and spongy. → Go to 11.

Y = young | M = mature | O = old

11	Plates are thicker than the cover of a paperback book. → Go to 12.
	Plates are not thicker than the cover of a paperback book. → Go to 13.
12	Upper branches and upper trunk have thin curls of peeling bark. → O yellow birch (*Betula alleghaniensis*) 106
	Upper branches and upper trunk do not have thin curls of peeling bark. → O black birch (*Betula lenta*) 108
13	Outer layer of bark is broken into irregular scales smaller than ½ inch. → M sugar maple (*Acer saccharum*) 100
	Outer layer of bark is not broken into irregular scales smaller than ½ inch. → Go to 14.
14	Layers of closely adhered scales are stacked together to form plates or blocks. → M river birch (*Betula nigra*) 110
	Layers of scales are overlapping and more randomly placed, not forming plates or blocks. → M black cherry (*Prunus serotina*) 216

Y = young | M = mature | O = old

KEY 7
Ridges and Furrows

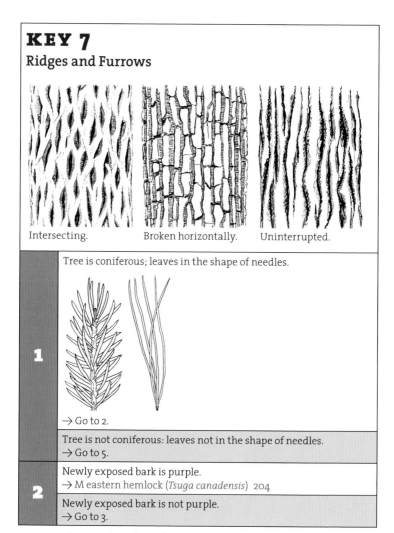

Intersecting.   Broken horizontally.   Uninterrupted.

1	Tree is coniferous; leaves in the shape of needles. → Go to 2.
	Tree is not coniferous: leaves not in the shape of needles. → Go to 5.
2	Newly exposed bark is purple. → M eastern hemlock (*Tsuga canadensis*) 204
	Newly exposed bark is not purple. → Go to 3.

Y = young | M = mature | O = old

3	Ridges are broken horizontally into blocks that curve away from trunk on top and bottom. → M pitch pine (*Pinus rigida*) 196
	Ridges are not broken horizontally into blocks that curve away from trunk on top and bottom. → Go to 4.
4	Outer surface of ridges is broken into scales smaller than a fingernail. → M eastern white pine (*Pinus strobus*) 200
	Outer surface of ridges is broken into scales larger than a fingernail. → M red pine (*Pinus resinosa*) 194
5	Upper trunk and branches are whitish, lighter in color than base. → Go to 6.
	Upper trunk and branches are not whitish, not lighter in color than base. → Go to 7.
6	Bark on base is broken into squarish or rectangular blocks. → M sycamore (*Platanus occidentalis*) 208
	Bark on base is not broken into squarish or rectangular blocks. → M bigtooth aspen (*Populus grandidentata*) 226 → M quaking aspen (*Populus tremuloides*) 230

Y = young | M = mature | O = old

7	Upper trunk has smooth, mostly parallel ridges (like ski tracks) separated by dark, shallow furrows. → M northern red oak (*Quercus rubra*) 150 → M pin oak (*Quercus palustris*) 148 → M scarlet oak (*Quercus coccinea*) 146
	Upper trunk does not have smooth, mostly parallel ridges separated by dark, shallow furrows. → Go to 8.
8	Cross section of ridge has alternating light and dark layers (like a wafer cookie). → M American elm (*Ulmus americana*) 240
	Cross section of ridge does not have alternating light and dark layers. → Go to 9.
9	Furrows are whitish or light gray, noticeably lighter in color than ridge faces. → Y tulip tree (*Liriodendron tulipifera*) 170
	Furrows are not whitish or light gray. → Go to 10.
10	Ridges intersect every 12 inches or less. → Go to 11.
	Ridges do not intersect every 12 inches or less. → Go to 20.

Y = young | M = mature | O = old

11	Surface is checkered by fine horizontal and vertical cracks. → Y & M black locust (*Robinia pseudoacacia*) 126
	Surface is not checkered by fine horizontal and vertical cracks. → Go to 12.
12	Ridges are subdivided into rope-like strands that appear to be woven together. → Y & M sassafras (*Sassafras albidum*) 168
	Ridges are not subdivided into rope-like strands that appear to be woven together. → Go to 13.
13	Ridges are flattened and burnished, as if they have been sanded and polished. → M butternut (*Juglans cinerea*) 164
	Ridges are not flattened and burnished. → Go to 14.
14	Sides of ridges are uneven, but smoothed (like river stones or sea glass). → M mockernut hickory (*Carya tomentosa*) 162
	Sides of ridges are not uneven and smoothed. → Go to 15.

Y = young | M = mature | O = old

15	Ridges are broken horizontally into the shape of upright or inverted V's or Y's. → Y & M black walnut (*Juglans nigra*) 166
	Ridges are not broken horizontally into upright or inverted V's or Y's. → Go to 16.
16	Ridges intersect every 6 inches or less. → Go to 17.
	Ridges intersect every 6 to 12 inches. → Go to 19.
17	Ridges are broken into squarish blocks. → M box elder (*Acer negundo*) 88
	Ridges are not broken into squarish blocks. → Go to 18.
18	Ridges are flattened. → M bitternut hickory (*Carya cordiformis*) 156 → M pignut hickory (*Carya glabra*) 158
	Ridges are not flattened. → M Norway maple (*Acer platanoides*) 92 → M green ash (*Fraxinus pennsylvanica*) 178 → M white ash (*Fraxinus americana*) 174
19	Ridges have parallel horizontal cracks. → M American basswood (*Tilia americana*) 236
	Ridges do not have parallel horizontal cracks. → M tulip tree (*Liriodendron tulipifera*) 170
20	Bark has vertically oriented, wing-like knobs and ridges. Cross section of trunk. → Y & M hackberry (*Celtis occidentalis*) 238
	Bark does not have wing-like knobs and ridges. → Go to 21.

21

Ridges are broken into sharply angled blocks with crisp corners

→ M chestnut oak (*Quercus prinus*) 142

Ridges are not broken into sharply angled blocks with crisp corners.
→ Go to 22.

22

Ridges are broken into squarish or rectangular blocks with parallel sides.
→ Go to 23.

Ridges are not broken into squarish or rectangular blocks with parallel sides.
→ Go to 24.

23

Faces of blocks are scaly.
→ M white oak (*Quercus alba*) 132

Faces of blocks are not scaly.
→ Y green ash (*Fraxinus pennsylvanica*) 178
→ Y white ash (*Fraxinus americana*) 174

24

Ridges are broken into roundish or oblong blocks not more than 3 times longer than wide.
→ Y & M black oak (*Quercus velutina*) 154

Ridges are not broken into roundish or oblong blocks.
→ Go to 25.

25

Ridges are wavy and irregular.

→ Y & M eastern cottonwood (*Populus deltoides*) 224

Ridges are not wavy or irregular.
→ Go to 26.

Y = young | M = mature | O = old

26	Bark has long, V-shaped furrows. 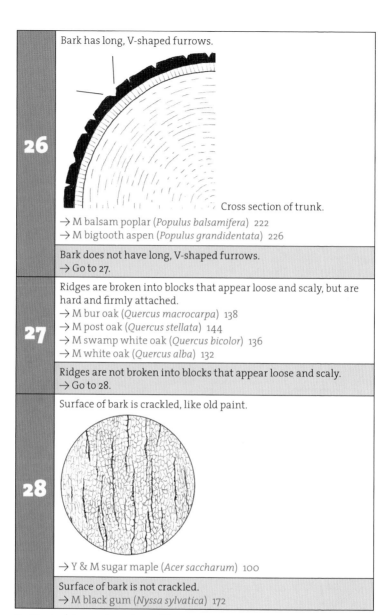 Cross section of trunk. → M balsam poplar (*Populus balsamifera*) 222 → M bigtooth aspen (*Populus grandidentata*) 226
	Bark does not have long, V-shaped furrows. → Go to 27.
27	Ridges are broken into blocks that appear loose and scaly, but are hard and firmly attached. → M bur oak (*Quercus macrocarpa*) 138 → M post oak (*Quercus stellata*) 144 → M swamp white oak (*Quercus bicolor*) 136 → M white oak (*Quercus alba*) 132
	Ridges are not broken into blocks that appear loose and scaly. → Go to 28.
28	Surface of bark is crackled, like old paint. → Y & M sugar maple (*Acer saccharum*) 100
	Surface of bark is not crackled. → M black gum (*Nyssa sylvatica*) 172

Y = young | M = mature | O = old

5 Bark Ecology

THE PRECEDING CHAPTERS offer a progressively narrowing focus on bark appearance, arriving at the small details that can be used for species identification: six different bark types, along with myriad characteristics within each type. Where does all this diversity come from? Why do species such as American beech (*Fagus grandifolia*) maintain smooth, unbroken bark for their entire lives, while the bark of northern red oak (*Quercus rubra*) and most other species cracks and thickens over time? Trunks with curly strips of bark, or those that gleam white in contrast to their brown and gray neighbors, make some species easy to recognize — but why are they so different?

A more complete look at the ecology of bark requires a broader perspective — of the entire tree and the environment in which each species has evolved. Drought, temperature extremes, fire, limited growing seasons, and interactions with other plants, fungi, bacteria, and animals all influence bark features. Bark ecology involves a complex web of energy production, thermal regulation, protection against infection and infestation, and associations with other organisms. Over time, humans have discovered many uses for the properties of bark that result from these adaptations.

Energy Production

Use your fingernail to scrape away the thin outer bark on a sapling, twig, or young branch from most species in the Northeast and you will uncover the surprisingly green cork skin (fig. 5.1). This bark layer contains chlorophyll and can perform, to a lesser degree, the same energy-producing photosynthesis as the leaves.

Fig. 5.1. Green, photosynthetic cork skin of an American beech.

Levels of photosynthetic activity depend on the amount of sunlight that penetrates the outer bark to reach this green layer. On the youngest twigs of some species, as much as 50 percent of available light reaches the cork skin. But for most species in this region, the mature bark on the trunk and branches is thick enough to block most or all sunlight. Although some light penetrates through cracks, furrows, and lenticels—which allow the gas exchange necessary for bark photosynthesis to occur—only newer growth typically collects sufficient sunlight for bark photosynthesis.

A small number of local species, however, maintain bark thin enough for sunlight to penetrate—even on the trunk. American beech releases its outermost bark layer as a fine, almost imperceptible dust. The bark of quaking aspen (*Populus tremuloides*) sheds a more obvious powdery bloom that can stick to your hands if you touch the trunk. On other species, such as paper birch (*Betula papyrifera*) and yellow birch (*Betula alleghaniensis*), outer layers of bark peel away in curly strips.

Supplemental energy produced by bark photosynthesis is thought to support regular cell maintenance in the trunk and branches, and can help trees to recover from partial or full defoliation due to insect infestation, storms, or severe drought. Production is especially strong in the spring and fall, when the trunk and branches are not shaded by leaves. The green cork skin of species such as quaking aspen and sycamore (*Platanus occidentalis*) can be active even in winter. Studies have documented the initiation of bark photosynthesis only 1 hour after air temperatures rose above freezing. Bark on the sunnier south- and southwest-facing sides of the trunk, where chlorophyll concentrations are often the greatest, can warm up considerably more than the surrounding air, making it possible to generate energy even when temperatures are below freezing.

Bark photosynthesis helps some species grow in challenging ecological niches. American beech tolerates shady growing conditions, and both quaking aspen and paper birch survive the short growing seasons at high altitudes and high latitudes—just as needles retained throughout the year help conifers grow in these locations.

Thermal Regulation

The outer bark's dead, mostly air-filled cells function much like the air-trapping fibers in home insulation, keeping the inside warmer or cooler than the outside. Outer bark protects not only against extreme cold and heat, but also from abrupt temperature fluctuations. Thick bark generally insulates better than thin bark, but bark density, color, and structure also play pivotal roles. When trees with outer bark of the same thickness were compared, the multilayered bark of eastern hemlock (*Tsuga canadensis*) was proven almost twice as fire resistant as that of balsam fir (*Abies balsamea*), which is more dense. Ridges, scales, plates, and vertical strips can function as radiator fins, dramatically increasing the surface area of the outer bark and helping to maintain an even temperature profile. These contoured barks also hold moisture, which is thought to slow the transfer of heat through the outer bark.

FIRE

The extreme heat of fire easily penetrates the thin outer bark of species such as American beech, killing sections of living tissue or even the whole tree. Species with thick, corky bark, such as northern red oak, can tolerate exposure to high temperatures for longer periods of time, but even they can be damaged or killed by hot, slow-moving fires. Evidence of fire may appear as a basal scar: a mark at the base of the trunk where damaged bark has fallen away and left the wood exposed (fig. 5.2). For trees growing on a slope, such wounds often form on the uphill side, where leaves and sticks accumulate against the trunk and increase the duration and intensity of exposure. (Note: not all basal scars are evidence of fire. The impact of a falling tree or branch can occasionally strip away a section of bark, while some basal scars, especially along roads, are caused by injury from logging operations or other human activity.)

Fig. 5.2. Basal scar of unknown origin at base of a white ash (*Fraxinus americana*). The injury occurred long ago; although wound cork was able to close the gap considerably, some wood is still exposed.

Levels of thermal protection vary among species and also can change with age. The length of time it takes for outer bark to thicken on a young tree frequently depends on the fire cycle—the average interval between fires—with which the species has evolved. For example, black oak (*Quercus velutina*), which typically grows in drier, more fire-prone habitats than any other species in the red oak group, also develops thick bark earlier than any of these relatives. The outer bark of pitch pine (*Pinus rigida*), the most fire-adapted species in the Northeast, thickens when the trees are still young and develops into deep, corky blocks that allow this species to thrive in dry, fire-prone habitats like Cape Cod. Pitch pine's outer bark also harbors epicormic buds that can sprout into new branches after a fire.

TEMPERATURE CHANGE

It might be hard to imagine sunlight, the vital engine of photosynthesis, as a potential threat to trees. But as an agent of rapid temperature change, sunlight can injure or kill sections of bark. In winter and early spring, when the low-angled sun shines directly on the bark of frozen, dormant trees, their south- and southwest-facing sides can warm to over 70 degrees Fahrenheit. As temperatures plummet after sunset, the rapidly drying and cooling bark can crack as it contracts around the still warm and expanded core of the trunk. If daytime heating is intense and long enough, portions of inner bark can be activated from winter dormancy; a subsequent drop in temperature—even from a passing cloud—can refreeze and kill them. An opposite type of damage can occur in summer, when trunks accustomed to cool shade are suddenly heated by direct sunlight after neighboring trees fall or are cut. Under these conditions, known as sunscorch or sunscald, affected sections of bark crack and eventually fall away from the trunk.

Some damage due to extreme temperature changes can be plainly visible. For example, frost cracks are longitudinal fractures that most often form on the south- or southwest-facing sides of the trunk (fig. 5.3). They are thought to originate from an already weakened point: a break in the bark, a crack in the wood, or a defect from an old injury. Frost cracks can close during the growing season—thanks to a new layer of inner bark (and wood, if the wood has been injured)—but temperature fluctuations in the following winter often reopen them. This repeated cracking and healing forms protruding vertical scars called frost ribs (fig. 5.4). Similar injuries (both cracks and protruding scars) can be produced by the drying that occurs in a prolonged drought.

Less extreme temperature fluctuations also can affect the appearance of outer bark. Moisture—often deposited as wet snow—accumulates in the crevasses of rough, textured bark, then expands as it freezes. Repeated cycles of freezing and thawing can, over time, force layers of outer bark to detach from the trunk. This weathering accelerates normal bark development in most species, where expanding wood forces outer layers to detach, but it can also transform a tree's appearance. On old black gum (*Nyssa sylvatica*), thick, rough blocks resembling alligator hide break away from the trunk, leaving behind sections of flattened ridges with shallow furrows (fig. 5.5).

OTHER ADAPTATIONS

Why don't all species in this region develop thick, corky, or contoured bark to protect them from fire and temperature fluctuations? For some, the benefits of thin, smooth bark outweigh the consequences. Resources for growth are finite; energy spent developing thick, rough bark cannot be devoted to other needs, such as food-producing leaves or nutrient-gathering roots. For example, quaking aspen—which has thin bark—regrows after a fire from vigorous root sprouts. Studies suggest that this strategy requires less energy than the development of more fire-resistant bark. Other thin-barked species, such as paper birch, counter their vulnerability to fire by producing large quantities of seed each year, helping to ensure their survival over generations.

Species that depend on bark photosynthesis have developed other methods of thermal protection. The light gray bark of American beech reflects sunlight, thereby reducing the chances of overheating. The thin, light-colored, and reflective bark of paper birch and quaking aspen also helps these species survive the short growing season and dramatic temperature fluctuations in northern latitudes and at high altitudes. Quaking aspen's pow-

Fig. 5.3. (*Above*) Frost crack on a balsam fir.

Fig. 5.4. (*Right*) Frost rib on a yellow birch. The frost rib's young, yellow bark contrasts with older, darker bark on the rest of the trunk.

Fig. 5.5. Weathered bark on the right side of this black gum contrasts sharply with thick blocks on the left.

dery bloom reflects sunlight so well that it was used by Native Americans as a sunscreen. Betulin, a compound that whitens paper birch bark, also seals in moisture to prevent desiccation on cold winter nights. Recently, despite its adaptations to temperature extremes, paper birch has suffered from a higher incidence of sunscald. Thought to stem from climate change, this condition has contributed to the decline of this species in the region.

Smooth, thin-barked species are also less prone to serious injury from lightning strikes. When lightning hits a species such as American beech, the charge tends to follow the rainwater sheeting down the smooth trunk to the ground, leaving behind little damage. Water retained by rough bark, such as that on northern red oak, is instantly converted by lightning to steam. The resulting pressure blows off sections of bark and creates a vertical scar. If wet bark conducts the charge through the bark to the xylem tissue the wood also splits, and if enough moisture within the tree is converted to steam a section of the trunk actually explodes.

Infection and Infestation

Like the exterior walls of a house, outer bark not only insulates against temperature extremes, it also protects against intruders. In general, American beech and other thin-barked species are easier to penetrate than species with thick bark like northern red oak. But just as doors and windows are the least secure points in a house, bark of any thickness or structure has weak spots — at lenticels, at cracks and furrows, and at branch junctions, where wrinkles bring the outer bark closer to the surface (fig. 5.6). Most harmful agents, though, gain entry through wounds created by numerous sources, including fire, sunscald, frost cracks, broken branches, logging damage, insects, birds, and mammals.

Breaches in the outer bark, from any source, open potential pathways for secondary invaders such as fungi, bacteria, and insects that would have been unable to penetrate the outer bark on their own. A chain reaction can result, where multiple stressors combine to damage or kill a tree. Environmental influences such as drought or poor nutrition lower a tree's resistance and magnify the damage caused by these invaders. In most cases, however, a healthy tree can overcome multiple infections or infestations through a combination of defenses and healing mechanisms.

Fig. 5.6. Wrinkles in the bark around branch junctions are clearly visible on thin-barked American beech, but often hidden on thicker-barked species.

Intruders that have penetrated the outer bark often leave visible evidence of their passage but, in some cases, only subtle clues remain. When insects bore into bark to deposit their eggs, they typically leave nothing but a tiny hole, and perhaps a little bark dust. After the larvae hatch, they burrow farther into the bark or wood, sometimes creating extensive galleries of hidden tunnels that can damage a tree's circulatory system.

Such small tunnels are the conduits of Dutch elm disease, a devastating infection. In the early 1900s, a European species of elm bark beetle was accidentally introduced to North America. These insects were carriers of a fungus to which native elms had little natural immunity. As the disease spread, native elm bark beetles visited infected trees and also began to distribute the fungus. The impact on American elm (*Ulmus americana*) was especially dramatic. The majority of large trees, including most of the stately elms that once lined the streets of many Northeast towns and that once dominated some rich-site riparian forests, died within 30 years of introduction. However, smaller trees still grow and reproduce in their native habitat.

Carpenter ants and other insects often enter through existing tunnels or other wounds, especially if fungal decay also has occurred. In search of these insects, woodpeckers — most notably the pileated woodpecker (*Dryocopus pileatus*) — strip outer layers of bark or even excavate wood. You can often find shreds of bark and wood on the ground beneath infested trees. Another member of the woodpecker family, the yellow-bellied sapsucker (*Sphyrapicus varius*), creates curiously symmetrical rows of holes in the bark of paper birch, American basswood (*Tilia americana*), eastern hemlock, and other species. The neat arrangements (fig. 5.7) are more obvious than the small, single holes left by bark beetles. Sapsuckers regularly return to these sites both to drink sap and to consume the insects that congregate there. This convenient source of sap also feeds ruby-throated hummingbirds (*Archilochus colubris*), fungi, and many other organisms. Red squirrels (*Tamiasciurus hudonicus*) practice their own version of maple sugaring; they bite through the bark of sugar maple (*Acer saccharum*) in late winter to harvest sap.

Fig. 5.7. Rows of holes in the bark of an eastern hemlock made by yellow-bellied sapsuckers.

Bark itself provides nutrition for many mammals, including humans. Native Americans dried the inner bark of eastern hemlock, eastern white pine (*Pinus strobus*), or slippery elm (*Ulmus rubra*) and ground it into flour. The inner bark of these and other species is still referred to in many guides to edible plants. Other mammals most often consume inner bark in winter, when more easily harvested foods are scarce. Porcupines (*Erethizon dorsatum*) perch in the upper reaches of sugar maple and other species and feed on inner bark, frequently girdling the trunk or branches. Sometimes they also strip bark at the base of a tree, especially American beech. Snowshoe hare (*Lepus americanus*), eastern cottontail (*Sylvilagus floridanus*), New England cottontail (*Sylvilagus transitionalis*), voles, and mice all strip bark from the bases of young trees, often leaving behind small teeth marks. Occasionally a tree is girdled and killed. In late winter or early spring, you may encounter old vole tunnels that lead through melting snow to a tree.

If the wood beneath the bark also shows sign of gnawing (fig. 5.8), it is likely the work of beavers (*Castor canadensis*) intent on felling the tree. They usually chew trunks and branches into small sections before stripping and eating the inner bark, and favor trees in the willow family (Salicaceae), such as willow, aspen, poplar, and cottonwood. Beavers that consume the bark of conifers such as eastern white pine and eastern hemlock—species at the bottom of their food preference list—have likely exhausted their choice foods in the area and may soon be relocating. Beavers may also girdle and kill conifers without eating their bark or attempting to cut them down. Consequently, they reduce competition for their more desired species.

Moose (*Alces alces*) and white-tailed deer (*Odocoileus virginianus*) also consume inner bark as part of their winter diet, using an upward motion with their lower incisors to scrape bark from trunks (fig. 5.9). Moose scrapes are often found on smooth-barked red maple (*Acer rubrum*) and American mountain ash (*Sorbus americana*), while deer frequently favor young eastern hemlocks. In the fall, male moose and white-tailed deer rub bark from small trees with their antlers. It was long thought that these rubs were intended to remove velvet—the skin-like covering—from antlers, but newer evidence suggests that they mark territory and perhaps display dominance.

Like deer and moose, black bears (*Ursus americanus*) also mark trees to announce their presence in an area. They strip sections of bark, sometimes quite aggressively, and often leave teeth and claw marks. Claw marks are particularly noticeable in the smooth bark of American beech trees (fig. 5.10), which bears climb in search of beech nuts.

PROTECTING THE TREE

Wounds in the outer bark are a regular part of a tree's life cycle, just as we inevitably suffer scrapes or cuts to our own skin. How do trees defend against the infections and infestations that result from wounds? Each species has evolved a combination of chemical and mechanical defenses to repel potential invaders, compartmentalize and isolate them, or kill them once they have penetrated the bark. Depending on the degree of damage, some wounds can be sealed over time with new bark.

Chemical Defense. Some of the chemicals in bark may be familiar to us, but their defensive functions in trees are less obvious. Many of these substances are the waste products from active cell metabolism, stored within the dead cells of the outer bark. We know that

Fig. 5.8. Beaver activity at the base of a double-trunked red maple (*Acer rubrum*), where both bark and wood have been gnawed away. Note the wood chips on the ground.

Fig. 5.9. (*Above*) Scrape marks from a white-tailed deer that fed on the bark of this young red maple.

Fig. 5.10. (*Right*) Claw marks left by a black bear that climbed this American beech.

Fig. 5.14. (*Left*) It took 10 years for wound cork to seal the bark on this eastern hemlock.

Fig. 5.15. (*Above*) Burl on the trunk of a black cherry.

may be specific to a given species, visible changes in the outer bark can help with tree identification. For example, the presence of target canker in red maples is revealed by a series of concentric cracks in the bark (fig. 5.16). These mark the annual cycles of the disease's progress and the tree's subsequent compartmentalization of it. Neither the tree nor the fungus seems to gain the upper hand, and this competition can continue year after year. Not all red maples are affected by target canker, but it is the only species in the Northeast that develops this distinctive marking.

The ridges and dark furrows at the base of a mature quaking aspen might appear to represent the normal maturation of its bark. But these features (fig. 5.17), which contrast sharply with the smooth, whitish bark on the upper trunk and branches, form in response to continued cycles of a fungal infection that enters through lenticels or wounds. The rough sections of bark accommodate lichens, which keep the bark wetter and aid the growth of the fungus. Defensive efforts against a fungus by gray birch (*Betula*

Fig. 5.16. In the Northeast, only red maple develops target canker.

populifolia) form triangles, or chevrons, of dark, rough bark at branch junctions. Similar responses could play a role in the formation of chevrons on paper birch and other species (fig. 5.18).

Despite its multiple chemical and structural defenses, bark can't protect trees from all attackers. As we have seen with American elm and American chestnut, an invasive organism—one for which a species has no evolved resistance—can decimate entire populations. The prevalence of beech bark disease perhaps best illustrates the domino effect that can be initiated by a simple wound in the outer bark.

The smooth, thin, light gray bark of American beech deters epiphytes, allows light penetration for bark photosynthesis, and reduces overheating by reflecting sunlight. But the bark has no defense against the beech scale, a tiny insect—smaller than the head of a pin—accidentally introduced from Europe in the late 1800s. These insects penetrate the thin outer bark to feed on sap; in the process, they inoculate the trees with a fungus that would not be able to gain entry on its own. The tree's initial attempts to compartmentalize the fungus create small, knob-like cankers (see

Fig. 5.17. Dark, rough bark at the base of quaking aspen results from defensive efforts against fungi.

Fig. 5.18. Chevrons of rough, darkened bark at branch junctions on gray birch.

fig. 5.12). Typically the fungus overcomes these blockades, forming larger, perennial cankers that leave the bark pock-marked, cracked, and often unrecognizable as beech (fig. 5.19). Breaches in the outer bark permit secondary infections from other, decay-causing fungi and allow infestation by carpenter ants and other insects. Pileated woodpeckers in search of insect prey cause additional damage. The weakened trunks of most infected trees eventually snap,

Fig. 5.19. An American beech with beech bark disease.

leaving a bare trunk less than half its former height. Root sprouts, which often emerge before the trunk breaks off, are typically re-infected before they can grow into mature trees. Although thicker outer bark protects some old American beech trees, beech bark disease is widespread enough to change the species composition in many forests.

Associations with Other Species

Not all of the relationships between trees and other organisms are predatory or parasitic; some are beneficial to both species, while others are neutral. Many plants and animals live on or within bark for some or all of their lives. The list includes microscopic organisms, such as bacteria and protozoa, as well as fungi, slime molds (myxomycetes), snails, slugs, birds, mammals, spiders, and insects such as springtails, ants, and beetles.

Fig. 5.20. Lichens and moss on a northern red oak.

Ferns, mosses, algae, lichens, and other epiphytes use bark as a growing platform. Although they do not leach water or nutrients from their hosts, epiphytes can still impair trees. In tropical climates, they can amass in such large numbers that they break branches or pull down the trunk. In the Northeast, epiphytes are less abundant but remain capable of blocking light for bark photosynthesis, clogging lenticels, or—when dark colored—contributing to overheating by absorbing solar radiation.

Epiphytes accumulate the most on species like northern red oak, with its thick, rough, moisture-retaining bark (fig. 5.20). Smooth, unbroken bark helps prevent epiphytes from gaining a foothold. American beech developed smooth bark as a tropical species, and maintained this trait as it became established in cooler climates where epiphytes are less of a threat.

On many species epiphytes are shed when the outermost layers of bark detach from the trunk and branches. Layers of outer bark slough off as a powdery residue on American beech and quaking aspen, and peel away on paper birch. Red spruce (*Picea rubens*) sheds outer scales, while red maple loses strips of bark. In densely populated urban areas, this adaptation has an additional benefit for sycamore trees: the peeling bark clears away pollution that would otherwise block gas exchange through lenticels.

Mammals and birds often utilize outer bark without significantly diminishing its protective capability. Red squirrels peel strips of northern white cedar bark for their nests, as do many birds, including Swainson's thrushes (*Catherus ustulatus*). Red eyed vireos (*Vireo olivaceus*) use strips from paper birch. Bats find shelter right on the trunk, roosting behind strips of bark on shagbark hickory (*Carya ovata*) and other species.

One study of bark samples from healthy American beech trees found fungi from twenty different genera, along with many species of bacteria and protozoa. Other research discovered fifty genera of fungi on healthy sugar maple bark. It is likely that some of these fungi and bacteria survive solely on exudates or detritus from their host, gaining both a place to live and a food source without causing harm. The powdery bloom from quaking aspen bark is said to contain enough yeast (a fungus) that it can be combined with flour to make sourdough bread.

Bald-looking patches on the trunks of white oak (*Quercus alba*) and other species are caused by a fungus that actively consumes layers of outer bark (fig. 5.21). This condition, known as smooth patch disease or patch fungus, apparently does no immediate harm, since it does not penetrate through to the inner bark. Because it reduces the thickness of the outer bark, however, it may decrease protection from temperature extremes or penetration.

Some bark fungi and bacteria can benefit their host trees by defending against pathogens. Some of these species colonize outer bark and out-compete other, potentially invasive organisms. Beneficial fungi that inhibit the growth of canker-causing fungi— or sometimes prey upon them—are often found near lenticels and other weak areas of bark where pathogens might gain entry. When trees, and therefore any protective fungi and bacteria that inhabit their bark, received adequate water, the activities of these

Fig. 5.21. Smooth patch disease on a white oak.

beneficial organisms were found to be most effective. This may be one reason why trees stressed by drought are more susceptible to infection.

Bark organisms also can help nourish their hosts. Rainfall washing down the branches and trunk carries minerals, nutrients, and bits of organic matter from epiphytes such as lichens and mosses, along with fecal matter from bark-inhabiting insects. This stemflow is absorbed by the roots and provides a small increase in resources to the tree. One study found that stemflow enrichment from smooth-barked American beech was less than that from red pine and eastern hemlock, both of which have rougher bark with greater surface area that harbors more epiphytes and other organisms.

In addition to impacting the tree itself, bark inhabitants interact with each other, creating networks of relationships. Slugs move

Fig. 5.22. Trails of grazing slugs on an American beech.

along the bark of American beech, leaving behind cleaned trails as they dine on algae that can block sunlight for bark photosynthesis (fig. 5.22). Tiny insects such as springtails and bark-lice feed on mosses, lichens, and some fungi that grow on bark. Such insects occasionally transmit harmful pathogens, but frequently do no harm. In fact, their presence may actually benefit their host tree by attracting spiders, ants, and other predators that can control populations of defoliating insects.

The interactions between bark and other organisms often happen at a level we can't see—or fail to notice—when we are among trees. Many of them await scientific study. The facets of interspecies adaptations and bark ecology chronicled here really only touch the surface—much of this complex web of interactions has yet to be fully explored.

As for the interactions between bark and humans, even a short walk in your local woods will provide encounters with many resources for food, medicine, dye, clothing, shelter, and other daily needs. And, most likely, you will pass by several potentially life-changing features of bark that remain undiscovered. A host of human uses for bark, including those already mentioned, are detailed in chapter 6.

6 Species

box elder (ashleaf maple)
Acer negundo L.
maple family — Aceraceae

Habitat
Floodplains or near water, often on sites that have been disturbed.

Notes
Often with sprouts growing from lower trunk.

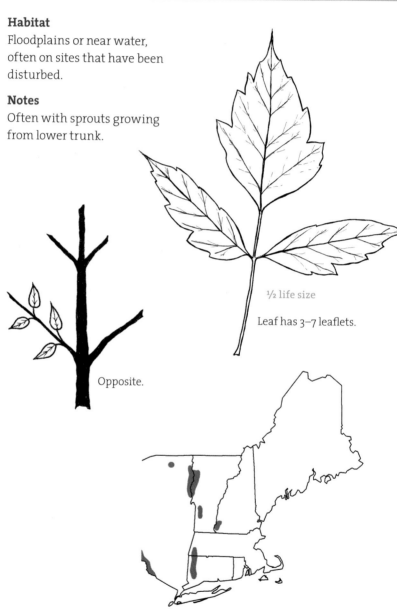

½ life size

Leaf has 3–7 leaflets.

Opposite.

Scattered populations elsewhere.

Young | Light gray-brown, finely scaly, with raised, wart-like, buff-colored or orange lenticels. Becomes rough and breaks into block-like segments, with lenticels still visible in furrows.

Mature | Remaining light brown to gray. Intersecting ridges develop and break horizontally into block-like segments.

striped maple (moosewood)

Acer pensylvanicum L.

maple family — Aceraceae

Habitat

Cool and moist, but well drained.

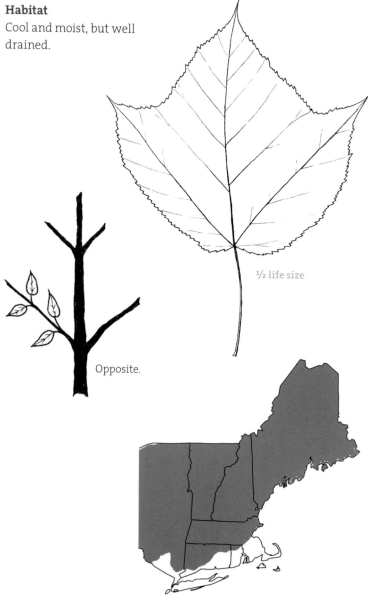

½ life size

Opposite.

Young | Smooth, green or greenish-brown, with long white or pale vertical lines. Diamond-shaped lenticels are often present.

Mature | Turning reddish-brown with dark, blackish vertical lines. Older trees develop rough bark, especially at the base.

Norway maple
Acer platanoides L.
maple family — Aceraceae

Habitat
Imported from Europe. Widely planted and has naturalized in many areas.

Notes
This species is sometimes considered an invasive.

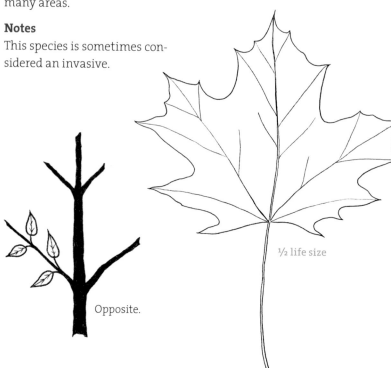

½ life size

Opposite.

Young | Smooth, brown to gray; developing narrow, vertical cracks with an orange tint.

Mature | Brown to gray, sometimes dark gray or blackish. Narrow, firm, intersecting ridges form diamond-shaped furrows.

Old | Ridges become wider and flatter. Diamond-shaped furrows are less pronounced.

red maple (swamp maple, soft maple)
Acer rubrum L.
maple family—Aceraceae

Habitat
A generalist, often found in swampy areas.

Notes
Bark similar to that of silver maple (p. 98), which has vertical strips that are more apt to curl away from the trunk and is less tolerant of shade and dry conditions. Bark is a source of brown dye.

½ life size

Opposite.

Young | (*Top, left and right*) Smooth, light to dark gray. Randomly distributed vertical cracks develop.

Mature | (*Bottom, left and right*) Gray to grayish-brown. Vertical racks become more consistent and form multiple layers of long, vertical, plate-like strips. Outer layers can be flaky. Strips remain fastened in the center but can detach and occasionally curl outward on one or both ends.

All Phases | Often infected by a fungus that causes the bark to crack in concentric circles, like a bull's eye. Not all red maples are affected by "target canker," but it is the only species in the Northeast that develops this distinctive marking. It is easiest to notice on young trees, but remains visible on bark that has broken into vertical strips.

A white-tailed deer has scraped away and consumed strips of bark from this young red maple.

silver maple (soft maple, white maple, river maple)
Acer saccharinum L.
maple family — Aceraceae

Habitat
Rich, moist sites on floodplains and bordering water.

Notes
Bark similar to that of red maple (p. 94), which has vertical strips that are less likely to curl away from the trunk and is more tolerant of shade and dry conditions.

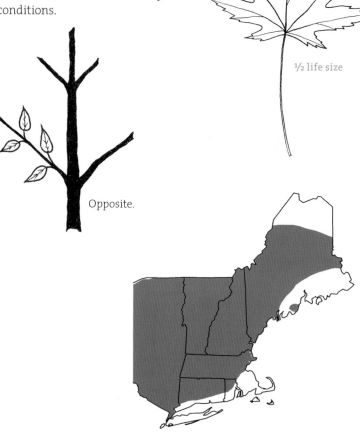

½ life size

Opposite.

Young | Smooth, silvery gray, sometimes with a brownish tinge. Randomly distributed vertical cracks develop.

Mature | Gray to grayish-brown. Vertical cracks become more consistent and form multiple layers of long, vertical, plate-like strips. Strips remain fastened in the center but often detach and curl outward on one or both ends.

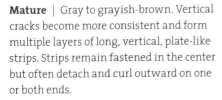

sugar maple (hard maple, rock maple)
Acer saccharum Marshall
maple family — Aceraceae

Habitat
Does best on moist, rich, well-drained sites but can grow on other sites as well.

Notes
Black maple (p. 104), which has darker, grayish-brown to black bark, is sometimes considered to be a variety of sugar maple. Black-green streaks are created when red squirrels bite through the bark in spring in order to consume the resulting sap flow.

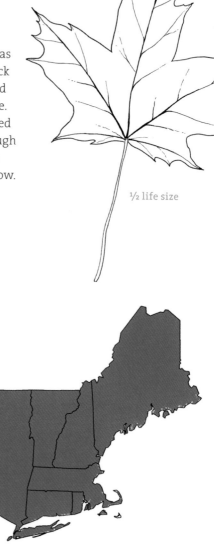

½ life size

Opposite.

Young | Gray or brownish-gray. The surface is finely crackled, like old paint; can be rough and somewhat warty-looking. Shallow vertical cracks develop; the bark between cracks sometimes breaks horizontally into irregular sections.

Mature | Gray to brown. Vertical strips separate from the trunk and often curl away on one side. The surface of these strips remains crackled. The strips continue to break into irregularly shaped sections and grow thicker and more plate-like over time.

Old | Vertical strips slowly detach and fall away, revealing more randomly broken bark with loose outer layers and without a crackled surface.

black maple
Acer nigrum Michx. f.
maple family—Aceraceae

Habitat
Found more often on moist sites than sugar maple.

Notes
Sometimes considered to be a variety of sugar maple (p. 100), which has lighter-colored bark.

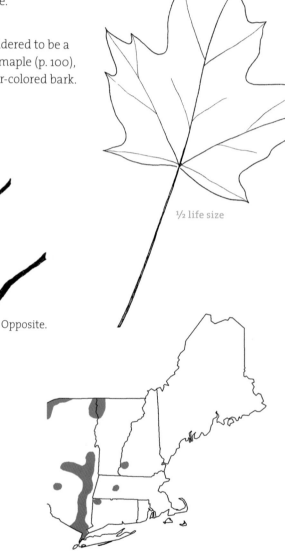

½ life size

Opposite.

Darker, grayish-brown to black, but otherwise
similar to sugar maple. Black maple is often
considered a variety of sugar maple, and
is not treated as a separate species in the
identification keys.

yellow birch (gray birch, silver birch)
Betula alleghaniensis Britton
birch family—Betulaceae

Habitat
Most often on cool, moist sites.

Notes
Bark is a source of yellowish-tan dye and of wintergreen oil, which is used medicinally and for flavorings. Bark curls are good for starting fires since they are highly flammable, even when wet.

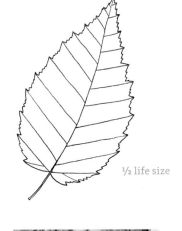

½ life size

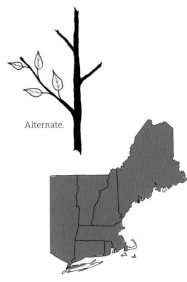

Alternate.

Young | Bronze or yellowish-gray, with long, thin, horizontal lenticels. Outer layers peel horizontally in thin, curly, papery strips. Inner bark (easily accessed on twigs and branches by scraping with a fingernail) has a distinct wintergreen smell and taste.

Mature | (*Above*) Color ranges from bronze to yellow to silver-gray. Lenticels become thicker. Curls of peeling bark are more abundant and may appear shredded. Inner bark retains its wintergreen smell and taste.

Old | (*Right, top and bottom*) Brownish-gray to blackish. The thin peels of bark fall away; lenticels are still visible. Thick outer layer breaks into irregularly shaped plates that eventually detach, revealing rough bark without horizontal lenticels. Over time this layer also breaks apart into rough, irregular plates and scales, also without horizontal lenticels. Inner bark retains its wintergreen smell and taste.

black birch (sweet birch, cherry birch)
Betula lenta L.
birch family—Betulaceae

Habitat
Moderate to dry sites.

Notes
Inner bark is a source of wintergreen oil, which is used medicinally and for flavorings.

½ life size

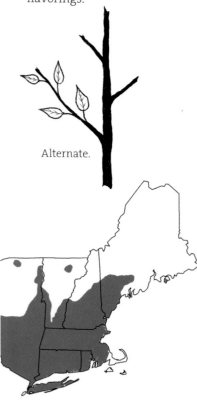

Alternate.

Young | Dark reddish-brown to almost black at first, turning grayer with age. Smooth, with long, thin, horizontal lenticels. Inner bark (easily accessed on twigs and branches by scraping with a fingernail) has a distinct wintergreen smell and taste.

Mature | Gray or dark brownish-gray to blackish. Outer layer breaks into thick, irregularly shaped plates that curl away from the trunk and eventually detach. The layer beneath is rougher, without horizontal lenticels, and over time begins to crack and break apart. Inner bark retains its wintergreen smell and taste.

Old | (*Right*) Outer layers break into irregular plates. Inner bark retains its wintergreen smell and taste

river birch (red birch)
Betula nigra L.
birch family — Betulaceae

Habitat
Wet areas along streams and lakes, in swamps, and on flood plains.

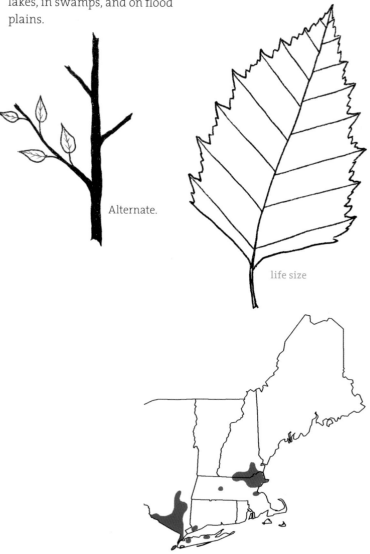

Alternate.

life size

Mature | Dark reddish-brown to dark gray. Closely pressed layers of scales form thick, irregular plates that separate from the trunk and often curl outward on their sides.

Young | Salmon-pink to brownish-gray, with multiple layers of loose, papery, curly scales.

Old | (*Right*) Layers of scales build in thickness to form dark, irregularly shaped blocks that are divided by deep furrows (especially at the base).

paper birch (white birch, canoe birch)
Betula papyrifera Marshall
birch family—Betulaceae

Habitat
A generalist. Not shade tolerant.

Notes
Red-eyed vireos (*Vireo olivaceus*) use strips of bark for their nests. Betulin, a compound that helps whiten the bark and keeps it from desiccating on cold winter nights, also provides chemical protection. It resists bacteria, fungi, and insects, and makes the bark distasteful to gnawing animals. A host of medicinal properties for betulin are being investigated for human use. Native Americans made containers, wigwam coverings, and canoes from the waterproof outer bark. Its antibacterial and antifungal properties made it ideal for food storage. Thin layers of bark were once used for writing paper.

¾ life size

Alternate.

Young | White, often with an orangish or pinkish tinge, with thin, horizontal, light-colored lenticels. Thin outer layers peel away from the trunk in curly strips.

Mature | White to creamy-white, with thin, dark, horizontal lenticels. Outer layers separate from the trunk in curly strips or sheets. Newly exposed bark is sometimes orangish.

Old | Sections of gray, rough, irregular bark, especially around base of trunk. Lenticels thicken and darken.

Heart-leaved paper birch (var. *cordifolia*), also called mountain paper birch, is a subspecies found on upper elevations in this region. The bark has a bronzish tint and peels in multiple layers, giving a more ragged look.

gray birch (white birch, wire birch)
Betula populifolia Marshall
birch family—Betulaceae

Habitat
A generalist. Not shade tolerant.

Notes
Dark, rough, triangular-shaped patches at the base of branches and at branch scars result from defensive efforts against a fungus (*Pseudospiropes longipilus*).

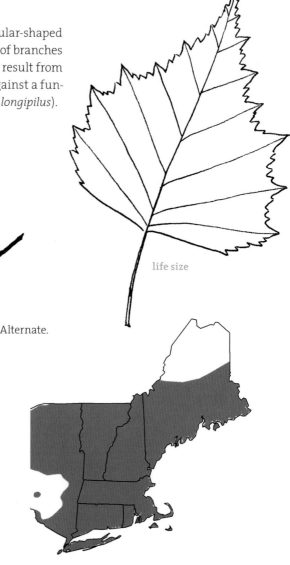

life size

Alternate.

Young and Mature | Smooth, white or grayish-white, with thin, dark, horizontal lenticels. Surface is chalky (not glossy), with little to no peeling. Dark, rough, triangular-shaped patches at base of branches and at branch scars form in response to a fungus (*Pseudospiropes longipilus*).

American hornbeam

(musclewood, ironwood, blue beech)
Carpinus caroliniana Walter
birch family—Betulaceae

Habitat
Rich, moist soils, most often
bordering water or wetlands;
highly shade tolerant.

Notes
A small tree, only occasionally
reaching 30 feet or higher.

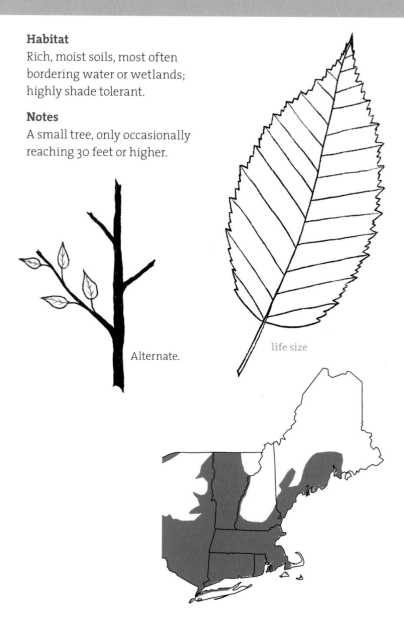

Alternate.

life size

Young and Mature | Bluish-gray, smooth and unbroken. Fluted, twisted trunk gives bark a sinewy, muscular appearance.

Old | Remains smooth and unbroken. Sometimes with light vertical lines.

hophornbeam (ironwood)
Ostrya virginiana (Miller) K. Koch
birch family — Betulaceae

Habitat
Dry, rich sites, most often
on slopes and ridges; highly
shade tolerant.

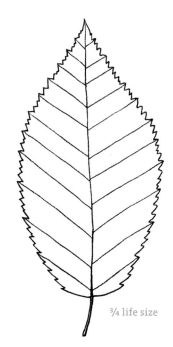

Alternate.

¾ life size

Mature | Vertical strips become thicker and less flaky, but remain detached on the ends.

Young | Brown to grayish-brown. Narrow, rectangular, vertical strips are loose on the ends. Strips are thin and easily rubbed off.

Atlantic white cedar (swamp cedar)
Chamaecyparis thyoides (L.) BSP
cypress family—Cupressaceae

Habitat
Wet areas—in fresh water wetlands, on floodplains, and along
small streams.

Notes
Evergreen.

life size

Mature | Grayer, with newly exposed bark more reddish-brown. Vertical strips become longer, thicker, and more fibrous, and continue to peel away from the trunk. Strips are often oriented in a slight spiral.

Young | Reddish-brown to ashy-gray, with thin, vertical, flaky strips that separate from the trunk at the lower ends.

eastern red cedar (red juniper)
Juniperus virginiana L.
cypress family—Cupressaceae

Habitat
Dry, sandy soils and rocky ridges. Often found on abandoned agricultural land.

Notes
Evergreen.

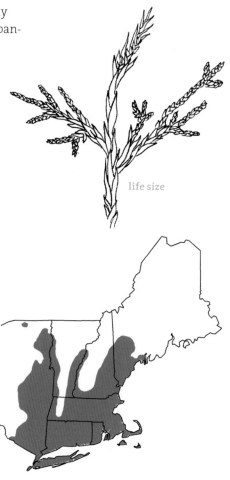

life size

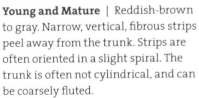

Young and Mature | Reddish-brown to gray. Narrow, vertical, fibrous strips peel away from the trunk. Strips are often oriented in a slight spiral. The trunk is often not cylindrical, and can be coarsely fluted.

northern white cedar
(eastern white cedar, eastern arborvitae, swamp cedar)
Thuja occidentalis L.
cypress family — Cupressaceae

Habitat
Mostly in wet areas.

Notes
Evergreen. Swainson's thrushes and red squirrels use strips of outer bark in their nests. In the 1500s, the native Iroquois showed French explorers how to prevent scurvy using a tea made from the bark, which contains vitamin C. The name arborvitae means "tree of life." Tough inner bark can be made into string or rope.

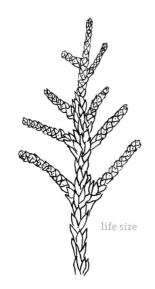

life size

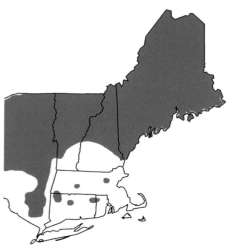

Young | Reddish-brown to gray, with thin, narrow vertical strips that often separate from the trunk at the ends.

Mature | Gray, with newly exposed bark brownish or reddish-brown. Vertical strips stiffen and continue to separate from the trunk at the ends. Strips are often oriented in a slight spiral; on older trees, they may intersect to form a diamond pattern.

black locust (false acacia)
Robinia pseudoacacia L.
bean family—Fabaceae

Habitat
Native to the central Appalachian and Ozark Mountains. Widely planted and now naturalized in this region. Often found in disturbed areas.

Notes
Twigs and newer branches have sharp double spines beside buds and single spines elsewhere. Inner bark is poisonous; it can kill livestock and make children severely ill.

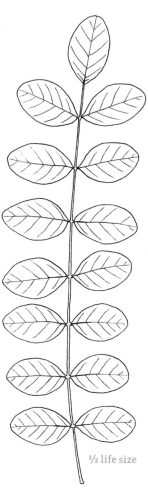

Alternate.

½ life size

Leaf has 7–19 leaflets.

Young | (*Left*) Rough, brown, with intersecting ridges and shallow furrows. Ridges checkered by fine cracks.

Mature | (*Below*) Darker, brown to reddish-brown. Furrows deepen, and checkering on them becomes more pronounced. Ridges intersect less frequently.

American beech
Fagus grandifolia Ehrh.
beech family — Fagaceae

Habitat
Moist but well-drained sites; highly shade tolerant.

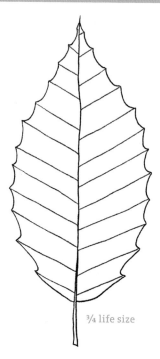

¾ life size

Alternate.

Young and Mature | Light gray to bluish-gray, becoming darker and mottled with age; smooth and unbroken.

Often with large, erupting blisters and cracks caused by fungi that initially gain access through punctures in the bark made by tiny scale insects. Referred to as beech bark disease, the infection frequently kills the tree.

Carving initials in beech bark is an old custom: *Crescent illae, crescetis amores* or "As these letters grow, so may our love." The initials shown here were carved 27 years prior to the photograph.

Lighter-colored trails show bark cleaned of algae by grazing slugs.

Claw marks from a climbing black bear.

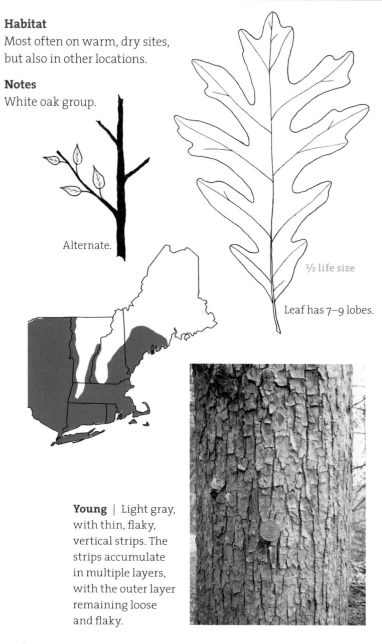

white oak (stave oak)
Quercus alba L.
beech family — Fagaceae

Habitat
Most often on warm, dry sites, but also in other locations.

Notes
White oak group.

Alternate.

½ life size

Leaf has 7–9 lobes.

Young | Light gray, with thin, flaky, vertical strips. The strips accumulate in multiple layers, with the outer layer remaining loose and flaky.

Mature | Light gray. Can appear whitish, and often with a reddish cast. Furrows form flattened ridges, sometimes with flaky surfaces, that are broken into somewhat rectangular-shaped blocks. Furrows are steep and narrow, with sides of blocks often parallel.

Old | Blocks are more irregular in shape and can break off near the base of the trunk, leaving behind patches of thin, flaky strips that resemble young bark.

Mature and Old | As trees age bark on the upper trunk and branches can look like shingles, with long, vertical plates that separate from the trunk on one side and on the bottom.

Smooth patch disease—found predominantly on members of the white oak group but also seen on elm and hornbeam—is caused by a fungus that consumes layers of outer bark, creating smooth, flattened sections on the trunk.

swamp white oak (swamp oak)
Quercus bicolor Willd.
beech family—Fagaceae

Habitat
Moist sites and wetland edges.

Notes
White oak group.

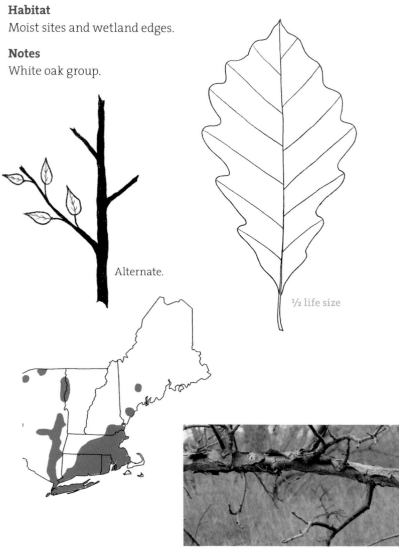

Alternate.

½ life size

All Phases | Bark on newer branches peels in irregular, papery scales.

Young | Light brownish-gray, with irregular, thin, loose, vertical strips.

Mature | Light brownish-gray, with irregular furrows and narrow ridges broken horizontally into blocks. Ridges are rough and scaly in appearance, but not flaky. On older trees, ridges can be loosely intersecting.

bur oak (mossycup oak, blue oak)
Quercus macrocarpa Michx.
beech family—Fagaceae

Habitat
Moist, rich sites.

Notes
White oak group. Bark similar to that of white oak (p. 132), which is lighter in color and has ridges that are less well defined and not as firm. Thick, fire resistant bark allows it to survive in fire-prone areas.

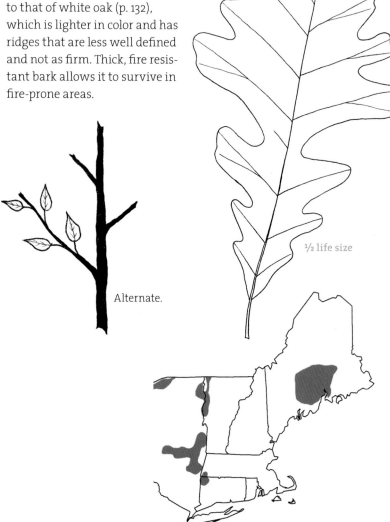

Alternate.

½ life size

Mature | Gray to brown; deeply furrowed. Ridges are rough, scaly-looking but not flaky, more flattened than rounded. They are broken into thick, long, irregularly shaped blocks and can be loosely intersecting.

Young | Light-gray to gray, broken into narrow, thin, vertical strips.

All Phases | Newer branches have corky, wing-like projections.

chinquapin oak (yellow oak, chestnut oak, rock oak)
Quercus muehlenbergii Engelm.
beech family—Fagaceae

Habitat
Dry, rocky or sandy sites.

Notes
White oak group.

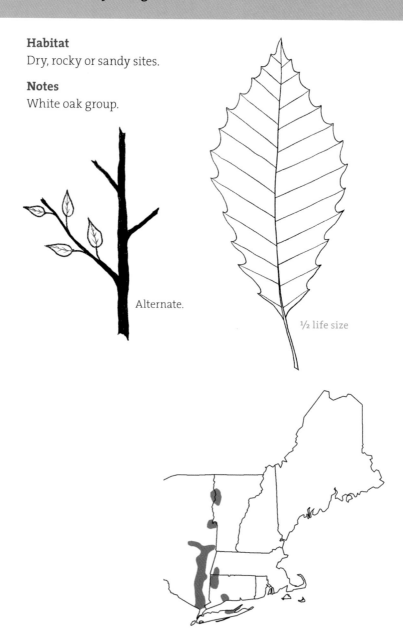

Alternate.

½ life size

Young | (*Left, above*) Gray, with thin, flaky, vertical strips that thicken and stiffen with age.

Mature | Light gray to whitish, broken into narrow, overlapping vertical plates.

chestnut oak (rock chestnut oak, rock oak)
Quercus prinus L.
beech family—Fagaceae

Habitat
Dry, rocky or sandy sites. Occasionally in rich, well-drained bottomlands.

Notes
White oak group. The thick, fire-resistant bark is rich in tannins.

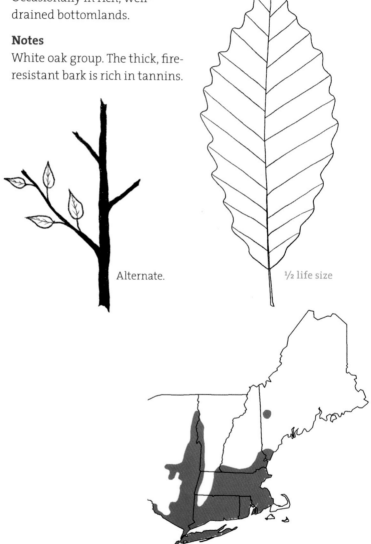

Alternate.

½ life size

Young | (*Above*) Dark brown to reddish-brown, with irregularly shaped blocks separated by shallow furrows. The blocks are smooth-surfaced at first, then roughen over time.

Mature | (*Right, top and bottom*) Dark brown to reddish-brown. Furrows deepen. Firm, mostly flat-topped ridges are broken horizontally into irregular blocks with crisp, square edges. Corrugated, angular in appearance.

post oak (iron oak)
Quercus stellata Wangenh.
beech family—Fagaceae

Habitat
Rocky, sandy, or dry sites.

Notes
White oak group. Bark similar
to that of white oak (p. 132), but
generally coarser.

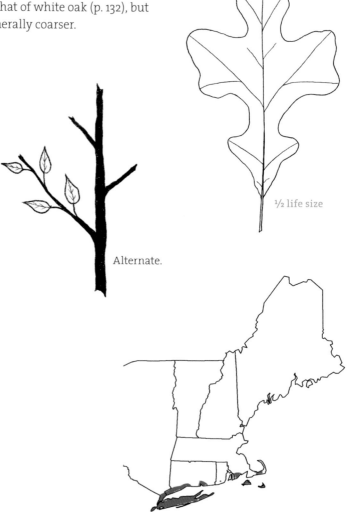

½ life size

Alternate.

Young | Reddish-brown to gray, with narrow vertical strips. Newer branches also have loose, flaky bark.

Mature | Darker and deeply furrowed. Ridges are rough, scaly-looking but not flaky, somewhat flattened, and are broken horizontally into irregularly shaped blocks.

scarlet oak (red oak)
Quercus coccinea Muenchh.
beech family — Fagaceae

Habitat
Mainly on dry, sandy sites.

Notes
Red oak group. Bark similar to that of northern red oak (p. 150), which has flatter ridges, and black oak (p. 154), which is coarser and has a more gradual transition between broken bark on the lower trunk and smooth bark on the upper trunk and branches.

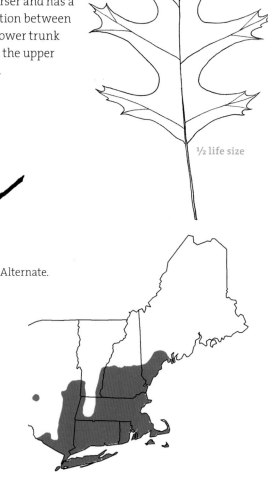

½ life size

Alternate.

Young | Smooth, gray-brown, with narrow, vertical cracks and sections of irregularly broken bark, mostly on the base of the trunk. Reddish inner bark often shows through cracks.

Mature | Becoming darker, brown to blackish-brown. Furrows and irregular ridges develop on the lower trunk. With time, ridges become rougher, somewhat rounded, and broken horizontally. Upper trunk remains smooth or has shallow furrows and smooth-faced ridges.

pin oak (swamp oak, Spanish oak)
Quercus palustris Muenchh.
beech family—Fagaceae

Habitat
Mainly wet areas along
swamps and waterways; less
often in moist upland areas.

Notes
Red oak group. Bark similar
to that of scarlet oak (p. 146),
northern red oak (p. 150), and
black oak (p. 154), all of which
have deeper furrows.

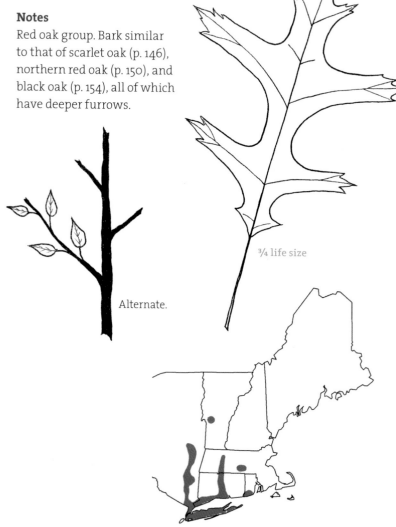

Alternate.

¾ life size

Young | Smooth, grayish-brown, with whitish, round or dash-like lenticels. Narrow, vertical cracks develop, often revealing reddish inner bark.

Mature | (*Above*) Cracks develop into shallow, rough furrows that separate wide, smooth ridges. Ridges at the base become rougher and broken, and are divided horizontally into squarish or irregular blocks.

Old | (*Left*) Ridges become rougher and break into irregular segments.

northern red oak (red oak, gray oak)
Quercus rubra L.
beech family — Fagaceae

Habitat
A generalist; found in all but wettest sites.

Notes
Red oak group. Bark similar to that of pin oak (p. 148), which has shallower furrows; of black oak (p. 154), which has ridges that more readily break horizontally into blocks; and of scarlet oak (p. 146), which has both of these characteristics to a lesser degree. Bark of mature and old trees is also similar to that of bigtooth aspen (p. 226), which has rough ridge tops that are close in color to the furrows.

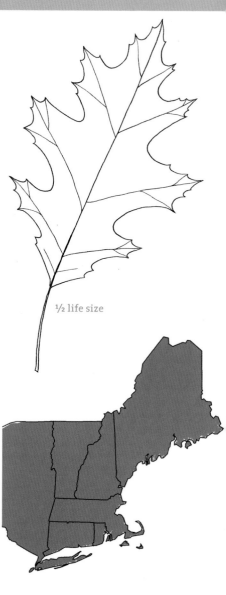

½ life size

Alternate.

Young | Smooth, greenish-gray to greenish-brown. Narrow, vertical cracks often reveal reddish inner bark. Small, buff-colored, round or oblong lenticels may be visible.

Mature | Rough, dark brown to blackish furrows separate smooth, lighter-colored, often lustrous ridges that are flush with the circumference of the trunk or slightly concave—so that the trunk appears like a fluted column. Over time the ridges at the base turn rougher and uneven. Ridges on the upper trunk remain smooth, often appearing like ski tracks. They may loosely intersect.

Old | Ridges become rougher and more broken, especially at the base.

black oak (yellow oak, quercitron oak)
Quercus velutina Lam.
beech family—Fagaceae

Habitat
Mainly on dry sites; sandy soils
or steep slopes.

Notes
Red oak group. Bark similar
to that of scarlet oak (p. 146),
which has a more abrupt transition between broken, furrowed bark at base and smooth
bark on the upper trunk and
branches. Yellow inner bark
has been used medicinally
and yields a yellow dye. Twigs,
when chewed, are bitter tasting
and turn saliva yellow.

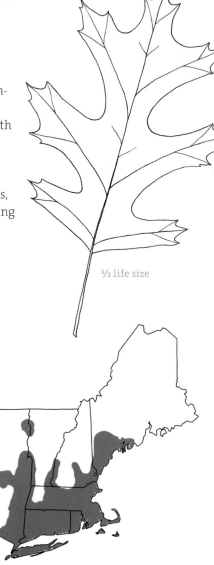

½ life size

Alternate.

Young | (*Left*) Dark brown to blackish; broken into rough, irregular blocks. Inner bark is yellow or yellow-orange.

Mature | (*Below*) Becoming darker, blacker. Rough ridges are broken horizontally into irregular blocks.

bitternut hickory (swamp hickory)
Carya cordiformis Wangenh.
walnut family—Juglandaceae

Habitat
Moist lowlands or rich upland sites.

Notes
Bark similar to that of other hickories—pignut (p. 158), shagbark (p. 160), and mockernut (p. 162)—which have coarser vertical strips and ridges that form at a younger age. Never loose and shaggy like pignut hickory and shagbark hickory.

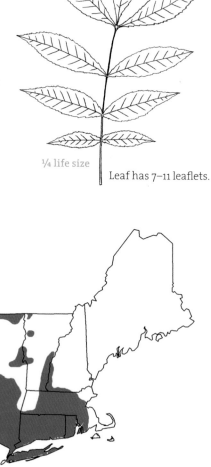

¼ life size

Leaf has 7–11 leaflets.

Alternate.

Young | Gray to greenish-gray. Yellow to orange vertical lines develop into narrow, vertical cracks. Bark remains tight and without multiple layers for many years.

Mature | (*Left*) Gray to brownish-gray. Tight, flat-topped, intersecting vertical strips give the appearance of a woven basket. Not loose or shaggy.

Old | (*Right*) Darker. Strips harden into tight, rough ridges that often form diamond-shaped furrows.

pignut hickory
(pignut, smoothbark hickory, red hickory)
Carya glabra (Miller) Sweet
walnut family—Juglandaceae

Habitat
Mostly on well-drained uplands.

Notes
Bark similar to that of other hickories. Bitternut hickory (p. 156) and mockernut hickory (p. 162) have tighter bark that is never loose or shaggy. The bark of shagbark hickory (p. 160) is looser and shaggier, especially on mature and old trees.

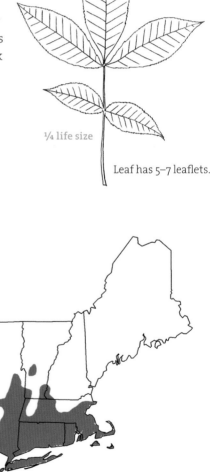

¼ life size

Leaf has 5–7 leaflets.

Alternate.

Young | Smooth, gray, with tight, vertical, orange lines or seams that develop into cracks. Bark between seams or cracks is crowned.

Mature | (*Top, above*) Outer layer breaks into intersecting, vertical strips that are cracked or broken horizontally. Surface of strips is crowned. The strips are tightly adhered, but can be detached at the ends and somewhat shaggy.

Old | Rougher, with less flattened, intersecting ridges.

shagbark hickory
(scalybark hickory, shellbark hickory, upland hickory)
Carya ovata (Miller) K. Koch
walnut family—Juglandaceae

Habitat
Dry, rich sites in uplands and valleys.

Notes
The bark of very young trees is similar to that of other young hickories—bitternut (p. 156), pignut (p. 158), and mockernut (p. 162)—but it cracks and forms vertical strips earlier than on these other species. Bats sometimes roost behind loose strips of bark.

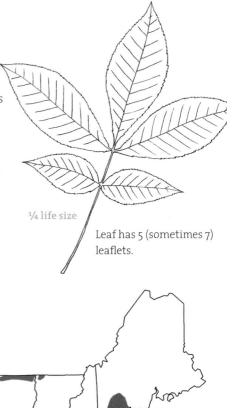

¼ life size

Leaf has 5 (sometimes 7) leaflets.

Alternate.

Young | Smooth, gray, with orange-colored vertical lines or seams that develop into cracks. Bark between seams or cracks is crowned. As the cracks deepen, irregular, vertical strips of bark begin to separate from the trunk.

Mature | Layers of stiff vertical strips accumulate. Outer strips taper to narrow, tattered-looking ends and curl away from the trunk, giving the tree a shaggy, shredded appearance.

mockernut hickory
(white-heart hickory, white hickory)
Carya tomentosa (Poiret) Nutt.
walnut family—Juglandaceae

Habitat
Mainly on dry ridges and hill-sides; occasionally on richer, wetter sites.

Notes
Bark of young trees is similar to that of other young hickories —bitternut (p. 156), pignut (p. 158), and shagbark (p. 160). Bark of mature pignut and shagbark hickories is looser and shaggier.

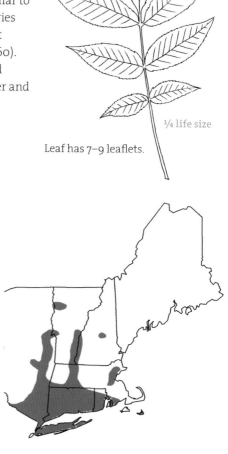

¼ life size

Leaf has 7–9 leaflets.

Alternate.

Young | Smooth, gray to brownish-gray. Orange-colored vertical lines or seams develop into cracks. Bark between seams or cracks is crowned.

Mature | Gray to brownish-gray, with rounded, wavy, intersecting ridges that are broken horizontally at irregular intervals. Sides of ridges are uneven but smoothed—like river stones or sea glass. Ridges are tight, never loose or scaly.

Old | (*Left*) Darker, rougher. Ridges are more broken and irregular.

butternut (white walnut, oilnut)
Juglans cinerea L.
walnut family — Juglandaceae

Habitat
Mainly on rich, dry or moist sites; occasionally elsewhere.

Notes
Dried inner bark was once used by doctors as a cathartic. Fresh bark yields yellow or brown dye, which was used extensively by early settlers and during the American Civil War. Juglone, the coloring agent in the bark, also inhibits the growth of many plants. Many trees have been stressed or killed by butternut canker.

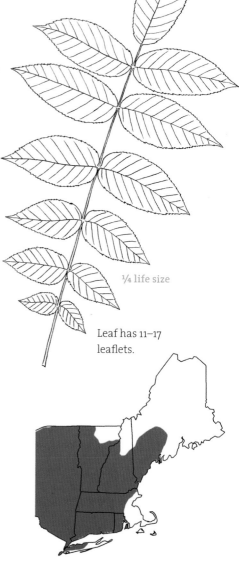

¼ life size

Leaf has 11–17 leaflets.

Alternate.

Young | Light gray and smooth, with rusty-brown to milk-chocolate-brown vertical cracks.

Mature | Cracks deepen into furrows, forming intersecting ridges that are gray and lighter in color than the furrows. The flat-topped ridge faces are smooth and burnished, often appearing as if they were sanded and polished.

black walnut (American walnut)
Juglans nigra L.
walnut family—Juglandaceae

Habitat
Rich, well-drained lowlands.

Notes
Fresh bark yields an orange-brown dye due to the presence of juglone, a substance that also inhibits the growth of many plants.

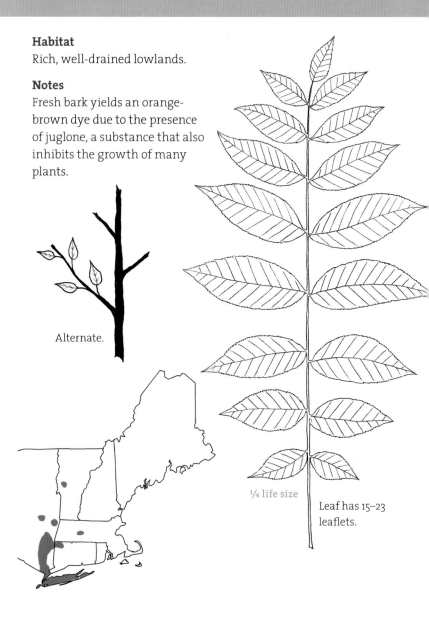

Alternate.

¼ life size

Leaf has 15–23 leaflets.

Young | Light brown or light grayish-brown. Flat-topped, intersecting ridges form narrow, diamond-shaped furrows. Ridges are broken horizontally at irregular intervals.

Mature | Dark brown to grayish-black; becoming thicker and deeply furrowed. Ridges intersect and are broken horizontally, often into sections shaped like upright or inverted V's and Y's.

sassafras
Sassafras albidum (Nutt.) Nees
laurel family—Lauraceae

Habitat
A generalist; found on rich and poor sites.

Notes
Bark, especially from the roots, yields oil of sassafras, which is used for perfumes, soaps, and to make sassafras tea. In the past, it was also used medicinally and to make root beer. The main flavor and odor component is safrole, which has been found to be carcinogenic in high doses. This compound helps protect the tree from damage by insects. Sassafras bark is thought to have been the first forest product exported from the New World.

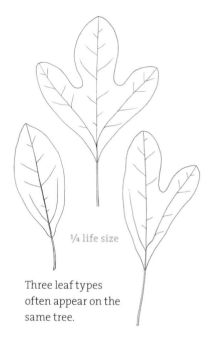

¼ life size

Three leaf types often appear on the same tree.

Alternate.

Young | (*Left, above*) Brown; cinnamon-reddish at the bottom of shallow furrows. Intersecting ridges subdivide into smaller, rope-like strands that appear to be woven together. Developing "axe marks" (blunt horizontal cracks), often across more than one ridge. Cut or broken bark is pale orange with a spicy and aromatic smell.

Mature | Turning more reddish-brown; appears to be washed with gray as age increases. Deeper furrows divide somewhat flattened ridges, which continue to subdivide into smaller, rope-like strands that appear to be woven together.

tulip tree (yellow poplar, tulip poplar)
Liriodendron tulipifera L.
magnolia family — Magnoliaceae

Habitat
Rich, moist, well-drained sites.

Notes
Bark is similar to that of mature white ash (p. 174) and green ash (p. 178), which have shorter and more regular diamond-shaped furrows. Acrid, bitter inner bark has been used as a tonic and a heart stimulant. Forest trees are tall, straight, and can be branchless for 60 feet. Sapsucker holes are common on older trees.

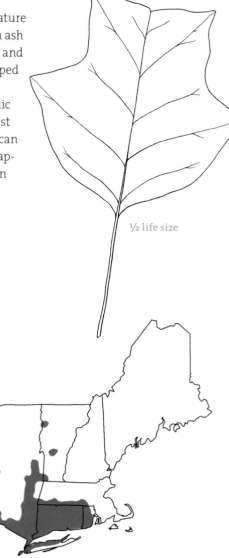

½ life size

Alternate.

Young | (*Above, right*) Ash-gray to grayish-green, with closely spaced, whitish vertical cracks that may be brownish or rust-colored at center. Cracks develop into whitish or light gray furrows with darker, gray to brown, flat-topped ridges.

Mature | Gray to brown. Ridges become rough, more rounded or peaked, and intersect to form long, diamond-shaped furrows.

black gum (black tupelo, sour gum)
Nyssa sylvatica Marshall
sour gum family—Nyssaceae

Habitat
Moist sites; often along streams or wetlands.

Notes
Sometimes considered a member of the dogwood (Cornaceae) family.

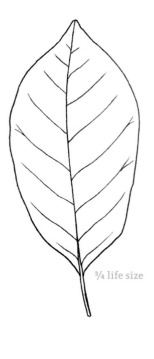

¾ life size

Alternate.

Young | Dark gray to brownish-gray. Divided into vertical strips with loose and flaky outer layers that become tighter and harder over time.

Mature | Brown to gray. Thick, rough ridges are broken horizontally into coarse, irregular or oblong blocks.

Old | Thick, rough blocks resemble alligator hide. Often with sections of shallower furrows and flatter ridges on one side of the trunk, where expansion and contraction from freeze-thaw cycles have broken off outer sections of bark.

white ash

Fraxinus americana L.

olive family—Oleaceae

Habitat

Mainly on moderate to rich, moist, well-drained sites.

Notes

Bark is similar to that of green ash (p. 178), which has shallower, often less distinct furrows. Lore has it that the name "ash" comes from the ashy-gray color of the bark.

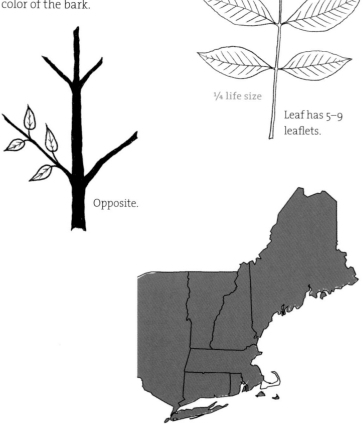

¼ life size

Leaf has 5–9 leaflets.

Opposite.

Young | Gray. Tight, squarish scales develop into shallow furrows and ridges broken horizontally into small, squarish or rectangular blocks.

Mature | Gray to brownish-gray. Rough, intersecting ridges form diamond-shaped furrows.

Old | Tops of ridges break off on sections of the trunk, leaving wide, flat ridges with crisp edges that continue to form diamond-shaped furrows.

black ash (swamp ash, water ash, hoop ash, basket ash)
Fraxinus nigra Marshall
olive family—Oleaceae

Habitat
Wet sites, especially rich
swamps.

Opposite.

Leaf has 7–11
leaflets.

¼ life size

Young | Light brown to gray, with soft, corky scales that can be easily rubbed off.

Mature | Darker gray to grayish-brown. Scales may build in thickness and become irregular and knobby-looking.

green ash (swamp ash, water ash, red ash)
Fraxinus pennsylvanica Marsh.
olive family—Oleaceae

Habitat
Moist or wet areas, including floodplains.

Notes
Bark is similar to that of white ash (p. 174), which has deeper and more distinct furrows.

¼ life size

Leaf has 5–9 leaflets.

Opposite.

Young | Grayish-brown. Tight, squarish scales develop into shallow furrows and ridges broken horizontally into small, squarish or rectangular blocks.

Mature | Rough, intersecting ridges form diamond-shaped furrows.

balsam fir (Canadian balsam)
Abies balsamea (L.) Miller
pine family—Pinaceae

Habitat
Moist, cool sites.

Notes
Evergreen. The sticky resin in the blisters can trap bark beetles attempting to bore into the bark. The fragrant resin, often referred to as "Canadian balsam," is used medicinally and as a clear cement for mounting microscope specimens.

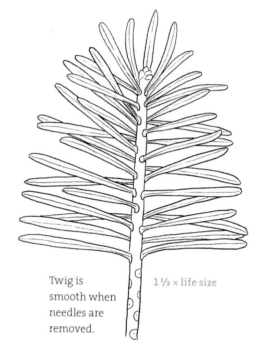

Twig is smooth when needles are removed.

1 ½ × life size

Mature | Resin blisters become somewhat rough. On older trees, especially at the base, bark becomes rougher and cracked, and can break into small, irregular brownish scales or plates.

Young | Gray to greenish- or brownish-gray. Small, dash-like lenticels are often visible. Raised bumps, referred to as resin blisters, contain a fragrant, oily resin.

All Phases | (*Right*) Resin oozing from blisters.

tamarack (hackmatack, eastern larch)
Larix laricina (Duroi) K. Koch
pine family — Pinaceae

Habitat
Moist and wet sites,
including bogs.

Notes
A conifer, but not an
evergreen; needles
turn yellow-brown
and fall off in au-
tumn. The bark is
rich in tannins. Por-
cupines frequently
strip the outer bark
and eat the inner
bark.

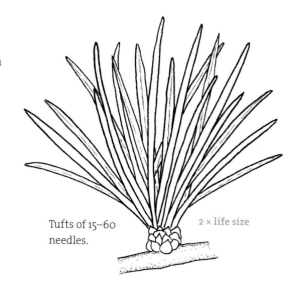

Tufts of 15–60
needles.

2 × life size

Young | Grayish to reddish-brown, with thin, irregular scales.

Mature |
Grayer, with newly exposed scales reddish. Scales are somewhat thicker and stiffer.

Norway spruce

Picea abies (L.) Karst.

pine family—Pinaceae

Habitat
Native to Europe and Asia.
Widely planted, ornamentally
and for reforestation projects,
and has naturalized in the
Northeast.

Notes
Evergreen. Bark is similar to
that of other spruces. Bark of
white spruce (p. 186) remains
unbroken to an older age, and
newly exposed bark is salmon-
pink. On black spruce (p. 188),
newly exposed bark is olive to
yellowish-green.

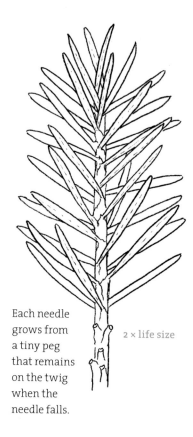

Each needle
grows from
a tiny peg
that remains
on the twig
when the
needle falls.

2 × life size

Young | Reddish-brown; finely shredded or with small, flaky scales.

Mature | (*Right, top and bottom*) Darker, reddish- to purplish-brown, with stiff, roundish scales. The outer scales become more irregularly shaped with age and begin to flake off.

white spruce (Canadian spruce, skunk spruce)
Picea glauca (Moench) Voss
pine family—Pinaceae

Habitat
A generalist.

Notes
Evergreen. Bark is similar to that of other spruces, all of which have bark that breaks into scales at a younger age. Black spruce (p. 188) also has newly exposed bark that is olive green to yellowish-green; on Norway spruce (p. 184) and red spruce (p. 190), it is reddish-brown. White spruce bark is eaten by porcupines.

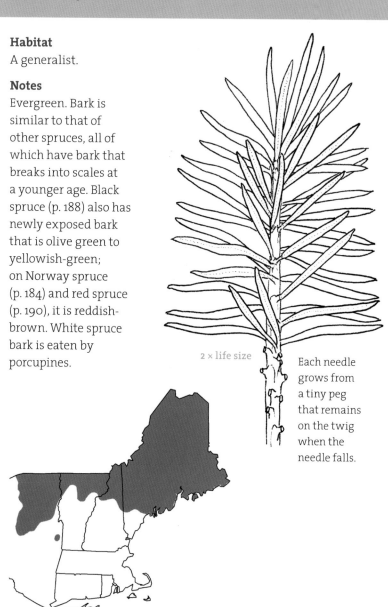

2 × life size

Each needle grows from a tiny peg that remains on the twig when the needle falls.

Young | Light grayish-brown; smooth or slightly roughened at first, eventually breaking into small, flaky scales.

Mature | Darker and grayer; broken into closely pressed, irregular, thin scales. Newly exposed bark is salmon pink.

Old | Scales can build in thickness. Newly exposed bark is salmon pink.

black spruce (bog spruce, swamp spruce)
Picea mariana (Miller) BSP
pine family—Pinaceae

Habitat
Mainly, but not exclusively, on moist, poorly drained, acidic sites.

Notes
Evergreen. Bark is similar to that of other spruces. White spruce bark (p. 186) remains unbroken to an older age, and newly exposed bark is salmon-pink. On Norway spruce (p. 184) and red spruce (p. 190), newly exposed bark is reddish-brown.

2 × life size

Each needle grows from a tiny peg that remains on the twig when the needle falls.

Young | Reddish-brown to grayish-brown; finely shredded or with small, flaky scales.

Mature | (*Right, top and bottom*) Becoming darker, with larger, irregularly shaped, thin scales. Newly exposed bark is olive to yellowish-green.

red spruce (eastern spruce, yellow spruce)
Picea rubens Sarg.
pine family—Pinaceae

Habitat
Moist to dry sites; usually in mature forests.

Notes
Evergreen. Bark is similar to that of other spruces. White spruce bark (p. 186) remains unbroken to an older age, and newly exposed bark is salmon-pink. On black spruce (p. 188), newly exposed bark is olive to yellowish-green. Red spruce bark is used to make spruce beer, and is a source of vitamin C.

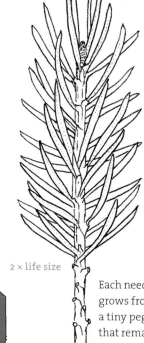

2 × life size

Each needle grows from a tiny peg that remains on the twig when the needle falls.

Young | Grayish-brown to reddish-brown; finely shredded or with small, flaky scales.

Mature | Broken into thin, irregular scales. Newly exposed bark is reddish-brown.

Old | Darker; scales build in thickness.

jack pine (scrub pine, gray pine)
Pinus banksiana Lambert
pine family — Pinaceae

Habitat
Sandy, shallow soils and rocky slopes.

Notes
Evergreen. Porcupines feed on the bark and cause deformed growth patterns. In this region, American starburst lichen (*Parmeliopsis placorodia*) is found predominately on the bark of jack pine and pitch pine.

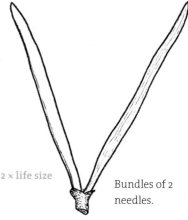

2 × life size

Bundles of 2 needles.

Young | Reddish-
to grayish-brown,
with rough, irregu-
larly shaped scales.

Mature | Darker
and grayer. Scales
build in thickness,
with outer layers
cupped away from
the trunk on top
and bottom.

red pine (Norway pine)
Pinus resinosa Aiton
pine family—Pinaceae

Habitat
Sandy, rocky sites and areas with shallow, less fertile soils.

Notes
Evergreen. Widely planted in central New England forestry operations from 1930–60 as a replacement for eastern white pine, which suffered heavily from white pine blister rust at the time. As a result, red pine is frequently found outside its native range and habitat. Black bears in this region often use mature red pines as marking posts.

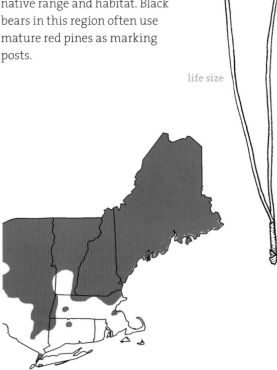

life size

Bundles of 2 needles.

Young | Reddish-brown to pinkish; broken into irregular, thin, flaky scales.

Mature | (*Right, top and bottom*) Layers of irregular, jigsaw puzzle–like, mottled red and grayish-brown scales broken by shallow fissures into irregular blocks. Surface of blocks is roughly aligned with the circumference of the trunk. Over time, blocks thicken and grow flakier.

pitch pine (hard pine, yellow pine)
Pinus rigida Miller
pine family — Pinaceae

Habitat
Poor, sandy soils and rocky sites.

Notes
Evergreen. Dormant buds can remain in the bark for years, then sprout when the tree is damaged by fire. In this region, American starburst lichen (*Parmeliopsis placorodia*) is found predominately on the bark of pitch pine and jack pine.

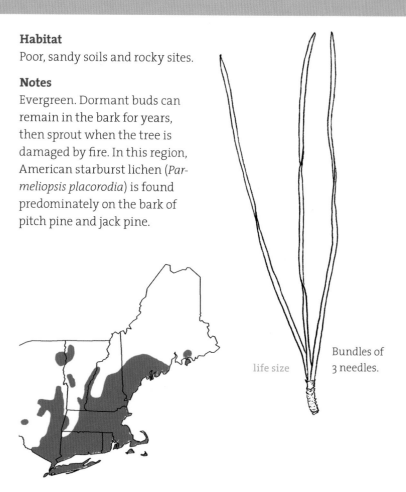

life size

Bundles of 3 needles.

Young | Reddish-brown to grayish-brown. Irregular flaky scales curve
away from the trunk on top and bottom.

Mature | Layers of scales divided by furrows are broken horizontally into irregular blocks that cup away from the trunk on top and bottom. Tufts of needles and short branches often grow directly from trunk.

Old | Blocks thicken and are more flattened. On the oldest trees, needles and short branches are mostly absent from the trunk.

eastern white pine (white pine, northern white pine)
Pinus strobus L.
pine family — Pinaceae

Habitat
A generalist; grows best in moist, sandy soils.

Notes
Evergreen. Native Americans dried the inner bark and ground it into flour. They also used it as a poultice for sores and wounds and as an expectorant for coughs and colds.

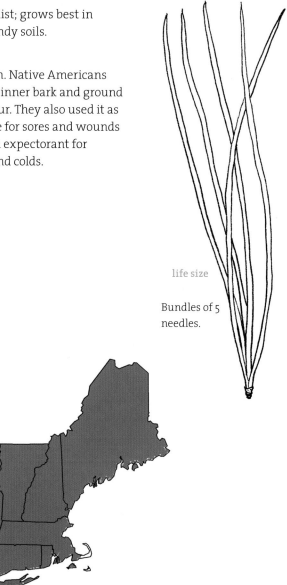

life size

Bundles of 5 needles.

Young | Smooth, gray to greenish-gray, with light-colored, dash-like lenticels. Turning grayish- to reddish-brown as it breaks into thick, irregularly shaped scales that turn out on the edges. The scales develop fine, horizontal cracks that are consistently spaced, like lines on writing paper.

Mature | Grayish- to reddish-brown. Layers of well-adhered scales form ridges that are broken horizontally into irregular blocks. The outer layer, still with horizontal cracks, begins to break into small, squarish scales and eventually flakes off. The new outer surface is broken into tight, rough, jigsaw puzzle–like scales.

Old |
Furrows deepen;
irregular, scaly
blocks begin to
cup outward on
top and bottom.

eastern hemlock (Canada hemlock, hemlock spruce)
Tsuga canadensis (L.) Carriere
pine family—Pinaceae

Habitat
A generalist.

Notes
Evergreen. In the past, tannins in bark were widely used for tanning leather; after the bark was harvested, stripped trees were often left in the forest. Bark is also a source of brown or mahogany dye. Native Americans dried and ground the inner bark for use as flour, as a thickener, and to stop bleeding. They treated diarrhea with bark tea. The inner bark is a favorite food of porcupines. Beavers only consume eastern hemlock bark as a last resort, but often girdle trees—possibly in an attempt to reduce competition for more-favored species.

2 × life size

Underside of needles has 2 white lines.

Young | Reddish-brown to reddish-gray; broken into thin, roundish or irregular scales, revealing cinnamon-red bark beneath. Warty lenticels are often visible in cracks between scales.

Mature | (*Below, left and right*) Scales build in thickness and are broken by furrows into ridges.

Old | Furrows deepen; ridges thicken and are often broken into irregular blocks.

All Phases | When firmly attached scales are removed, their undersides—and the newly exposed bark— are reddish-purple.

Eastern hemlock is the only species in the Northeast on which wound cork—produced to seal gaps in the bark—grows in annual increments that can be counted to determine the age of a wound. It took 10 years to seal the breach on this trunk.

sycamore (buttonwood, American sycamore, American planetree)
Platanus occidentalis L.
sycamore family — Platanaceae

Habitat
Rich lowlands as well as poorly drained sites.

Notes
Hearty and often planted in dense urban areas. The shedding of outer bark layers clears away pollution that could block gas exchange through the lenticels.

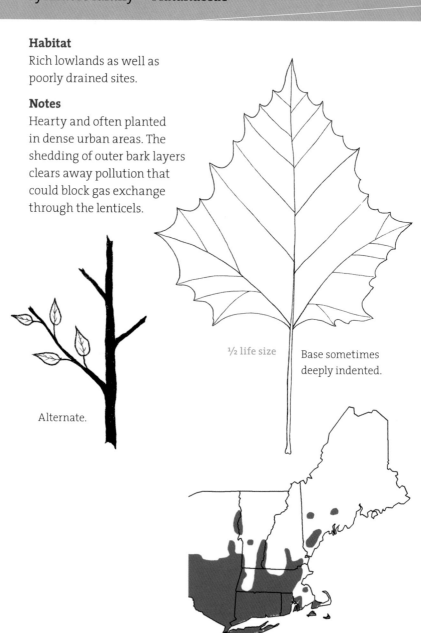

½ life size

Base sometimes deeply indented.

Alternate.

Young | Jigsaw puzzle–like scales or plates flake off and reveal the smooth white, creamy, or greenish bark beneath. Alternating layers of different colors can create a camouflage effect.

Mature | (*Right*) Layers of small, brownish scales build in thickness on the lower and middle portions of the trunk. Patches of smooth, lighter-colored, underlying bark are often visible.

Old | (*Below*) Becoming tighter and less scaly. Grayish-brown, flat-topped ridges are separated by steep, narrow furrows and broken horizontally into blocks. The sides of the blocks are almost parallel.

All Phases | Upper trunk and branches with smooth, whitish bark.

downy serviceberry (shadbush, juneberry)
Amelanchier arborea (Michx. f.) Fern
rose family—Rosaceae

Habitat
A generalist.

Notes
A small tree, rarely reaching
more than 40 feet in height.

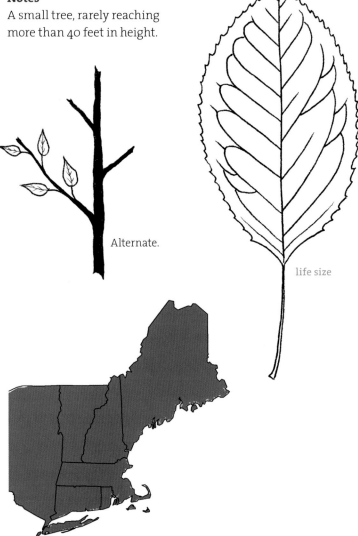

Alternate.

life size

Young | Smooth, light gray, with dark vertical lines.

Mature | Dark lines develop into long, blackened, vertical cracks.

Old | Sections of smooth bark between the cracks become blackened and rough, especially near the base.

pin cherry (fire cherry, bird cherry)
Prunus pensylvanica L.f.
rose family — Rosaceae

Habitat
Recently disturbed sites such as logged areas, burns, and blowdowns.

Notes
A small tree; infrequently reaching 30 to 40 feet in height.

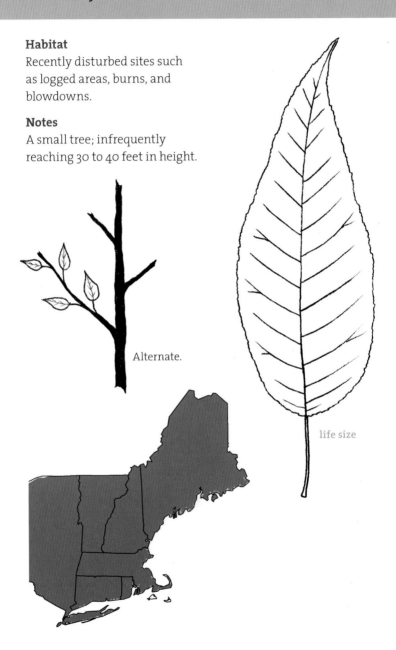

Alternate.

life size

Young | Smooth, reddish-brown; with warty, orange, horizontal lenticels.

Mature | Lenticels rougher and darker; sometimes peeling in narrow, horizontal, papery strips. Bark can become roughened at the base.

black cherry (wild black cherry, rum cherry)
Prunus serotina Ehrh.
rose family—Rosaceae

Habitat
A generalist.

Notes
Chemicals in the bark produce
a bitter almond scent and ward
off browsers. Bark extracts
yield hydrocyanic (prussic) acid,
which has long been used in
cough medicines, expectorants,
and to sooth sore throats.

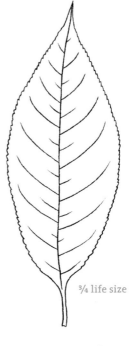

¾ life size

Alternate.

Young | Smooth, reddish-brown to grayish-brown, with gray, horizontal lenticels. Inner bark (easily accessed on twigs and branches by scraping with a fingernail) has a distinct bitter almond smell.

Mature | Smooth bark breaks into scales that are curled outward on the sides. The outer scales begin to flake off, revealing smaller, darker, irregularly shaped scales without prominent lenticels.

Old | Layers of reddish-brown to blackish scales with upturned edges. Scales appear like burnt cornflakes.

American mountain ash (roundwood, dogberry)
Sorbus americana Marshall
rose family—Rosaceae

Habitat
Cool, moist, high-elevation sites.

Notes
Bark is similar to that of showy mountain ash (p. 220), which is more greenish- or golden-brown. A small tree, rarely reaching more than 30 feet in height. The inner bark is astringent and is used medicinally. Bark is heavily browsed by moose.

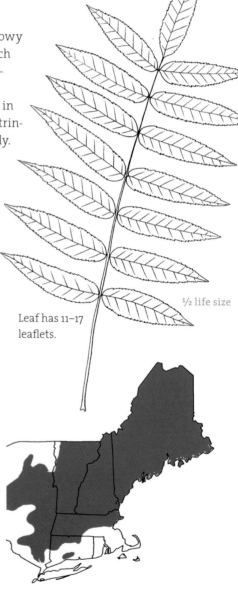

½ life size

Leaf has 11–17 leaflets.

Alternate.

Young | Smooth, gray. Horizontal lenticels are buff-colored to orange, with borders that protrude from the bark, sometimes appearing like lips.

Mature | (*Right, top and bottom*) Lenticels remain prominent. Irregular patches of cracked and peeling bark develop with age, especially at the base.

showy mountain ash (dogberry)
Sorbus decora (Sarg.) C. K. Schneider
rose family — Rosaceae

Habitat
Most often on rocky sites near
water, but also on other cool,
moist sites.

Notes
Bark is similar to that of
American mountain ash
(p. 218), which is grayer, not
as greenish-gray or golden
brown.

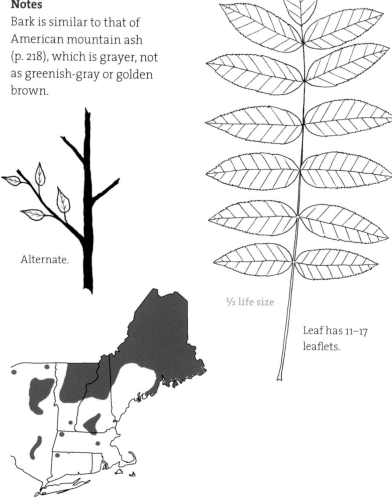

Alternate.

½ life size

Leaf has 11–17
leaflets.

Mature | Lenticels remain prominent. Irregular patches of cracked and peeling bark develop with age, especially at the base.

Young | Smooth, greenish-gray to golden-brown. The borders of horizontal lenticels protrude from the bark, sometimes appearing like lips.

balsam poplar (tacmahac, balm of Gilead)
Populus balsamifera L.
willow family—Salicaceae

Habitat
Moist sites.

Notes
Salicin, a compound found in the inner bark that deters bacteria, fungi, and insects, is also used as a pain reliever and is the precursor to synthetically produced aspirin.

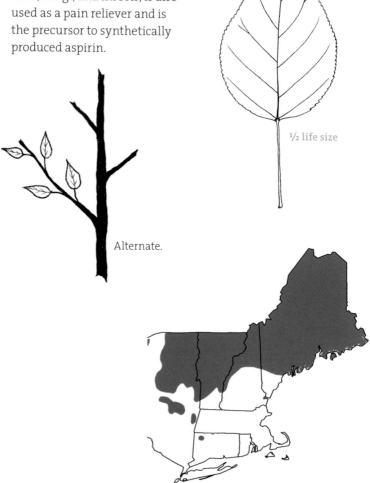

½ life size

Alternate.

Young | Smooth, greenish-brown to greenish-gray, often with a reddish tinge. Scattered, diamond-shaped lenticels develop over time into vertical cracks.

Mature | Darker, grayer. Vertical cracks develop into narrow, V-shaped furrows and firm, flattened ridges. Furrows form mainly on the lower trunk. Ridges eventually become uneven and broken.

eastern cottonwood
(Carolina poplar, southern cottonwood)
Populus deltoides Marshall
willow family—Salicaceae

Habitat
Rich, moist sites, most often bordering water.

Notes
Fishermen have used thick blocks of bark as floats for their nets.

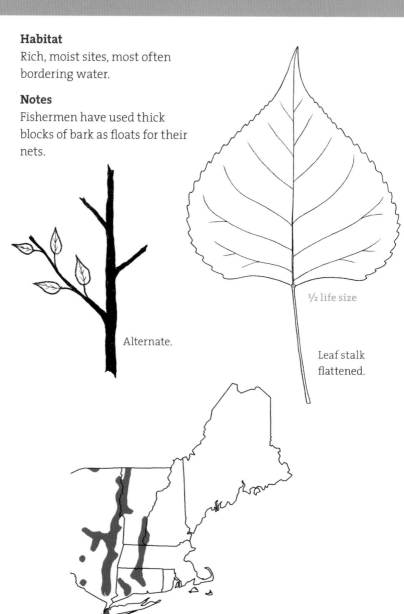

Alternate.

½ life size

Leaf stalk flattened.

Young | (*Left, above*) Gray to brownish-gray; shallowly furrowed. Rough, wavy ridges are broken horizontally into variably shaped blocks. The upper trunk and branches are smooth, yellowish-gray, and typically lighter in color than the lower trunk.

Mature | More deeply furrowed. Ridges are rougher and broken into irregular blocks that often resemble puzzle pieces.

Old | Furrows steeper; ridges more rounded.

bigtooth aspen (largetooth aspen, poplar)
Populus grandidentata Michx.
willow family — Salicaceae

Habitat
A generalist; found most often on sandy sites.

Notes
Bark is similar to that of quaking aspen (p. 230), which is lighter and more whitish when young and has furrows darker than ridge tops when mature. Also similar to bark of mature northern red oak (p. 150), which is not distinctively lighter on the upper trunk and branches. The bitter inner bark was once used as a quinine substitute and contains salicin, which deters bacteria, fungi, and insects. The compound is also used as a pain reliever and is the precursor to synthetically produced aspirin. The inner bark is favorite food of beaver and is often browsed by snowshoe hare.

½ life size

Leaf stalk flattened.

Alternate.

Young | Smooth, tan to yellowish- or greenish-gray; often with an orange cast. Diamond-shaped lenticels on the lower trunk join together to form rough, uneven patches and vertical cracks.

Mature | Darker; brown to gray. Furrows, often with orangish inner bark showing at the base, divide flattened ridges.

Old | Furrows deepen; ridges become rougher and more rounded.

All Phases | Upper trunk and branches retain smooth and light-colored bark.

quaking aspen (trembling aspen, golden aspen, poplar)
Populus tremuloides Michx.
willow family—Salicaceae

Habitat
A generalist.

Notes
Bark is similar to that of big-tooth aspen (p. 226), which is more yellow or gray when young and has furrows and ridges similar in color when mature. Thick and furrowed bark at the base of the trunk forms in response to a fungus that penetrates through lenticels or wounds. The bitter inner bark was once used as a quinine substitute and contains salicin, which deters bacteria, fungi, and insects. The compound is also used as a pain reliever and is the precursor to synthetically produced aspirin. The powdery residue on the outer bark (which can stick to your hands if you touch the trunk) helps regulate temperature extremes by reflecting sunlight, and was used by Native Americans as a sunscreen. This powder is said to contain enough naturally occurring yeast that it can be used to make sourdough bread. The inner bark is a favorite food of beaver and is often browsed by snowshoe hare.

½ life size

Leaf stalk flattened.

Alternate.

Young | Smooth, whitish; can be creamy yellow to light green. Often with raised horizontal bands, and sometimes showing horizontal or diamond-shaped lenticels. Outer surface typically with a powdery or chalky residue, or bloom.

Mature | Turning grayish-brown. Dark, blackish furrows develop, especially at the base, dividing lighter-colored, flattened, often intersecting ridges.

All Phases | (*Facing page*) Upper trunk and branches retain smooth and light-colored bark

willow

Salix spp.

willow family—Salicaceae

Habitat
Moist sites bordering water or wetlands.

Notes
Four species of willow in this region grow taller than 30 feet. Since their bark characteristics are similar and they are likely hybridizers, they are described together here. Black willow (*Salix nigra*) is native; crack willow (*Salix fragilis*), white willow (*Salix alba*), and weeping willow (*Salix babylonica*) are nonnative trees that have become naturalized. Salicin in the inner bark deters bacteria, fungi, and insects. The compound is also used as a pain reliever and is the precursor to synthetically produced aspirin.

¾ life size

Alternate.

Young | Dark brown to blackish. Loose, scaly, vertical strips or ridges appear soft but are hard, brittle, and break apart easily.

Mature | (*Right, top and bottom*) Brown to blackish. With vertical strips, often loose and flaky, or with ridges that may intersect. On old trees, bark becomes especially cracked and broken-looking. Trunk sprouting is common.

American basswood (American linden)
Tilia americana L.
basswood family — Tiliaceae

Habitat
Moist, rich sites; most often on slopes.

Notes
Fibers from the inner bark have long been used to make cord, fishnets, mats, and baskets.

Alternate.

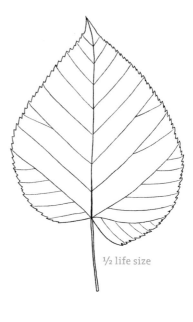

½ life size

Young | Light gray to light brown; broken by vertical cracks. Surface of bark between vertical cracks has horizontal, hairline cracks.

Mature | Gray to brown. Narrow furrows form long, flattened ridges with parallel edges. Ridge surfaces broken horizontally by hairline cracks, often into squarish segments. Ridges often loosely intersect.

Old | (*Right*) Ridges intersect more distinctly and often curve around branches or old branch junctions.

hackberry (sugarberry, nettletree)
Celtis occidentalis L.
elm family—Ulmaceae

Habitat
Mostly on floodplains.

Notes
Exudes gum, similar to that of cherry trees, that protects wounds from infection and infestation.

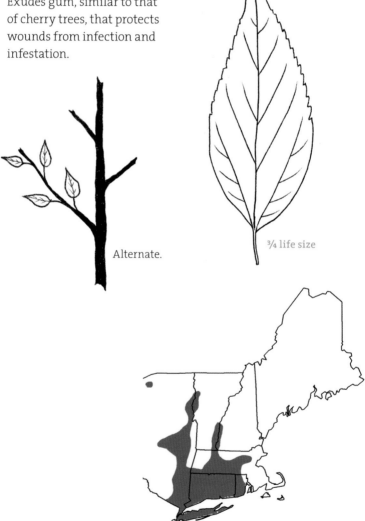

Alternate.

¾ life size

Young and Mature | (*Above, right*) Gray to light brown. Narrow, wing-like, corky knobs and ridges extend perpendicularly from the otherwise smooth trunk in vertical rows.

Old | Irregular knobs and ridges become more flattened and closely spaced.

American elm (white elm, soft elm)
Ulmus americana L.
elm family—Ulmaceae

Habitat
Rich, moist sites.

Notes
Dutch elm disease—a fungus accidentally introduced in the early 1900s and spread by bark beetles—has killed most large trees, including those that once lined the streets of many towns in this region. Iroquois Indians of western New York State used the bark for canoes and twisted its fibers into rope. Settlers made ox whips by peeling strips of bark and braiding them.

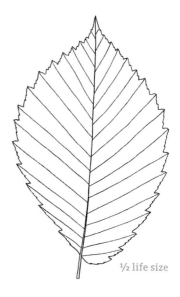

½ life size

Alternate.

Young | (*Above, right*) Mottled brown to grayish-brown; soft, spongy, with vertical strips or scales.

Mature | Scaly vertical strips may persist; most often thicker, rougher, with intersecting ridges that form long, diamond-shaped furrows.

Old | (*Above*) Ridges harder, deeper; long, diamond-shaped furrows more pronounced.

All Phases | (*Right*) Once the bark thickens, a cross section shows alternating, buff-colored and reddish-brown layers, like a wafer cookie.

slippery elm (red elm, moose elm, soft elm)
Ulmus rubra Muhl.
elm family—Ulmaceae

Habitat
Mainly on rich, moist sites;
sometimes on drier sites.

Notes
Also susceptible to Dutch elm
disease. Bark is similar to that
of American elm (p. 240), which
has alternating light and dark
layers. The mucilaginous inner
bark, which tastes like licorice,
has long been used as a sore-
throat and fever remedy and
to quench thirst. It was also
taken as a scurvy preventative.
Native Americans dried the
inner bark and ground it into
flour or twisted its fibers into
laces. It is also a favorite food of
porcupines.

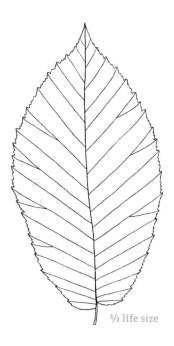

½ life size

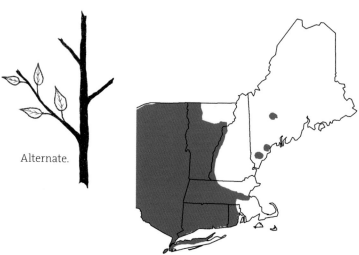

Alternate.

Mature | Ash-gray to dark reddish-brown. Vertical strips often separate from the trunk on one side and turn rougher, harder.

Young | Ash-gray to reddish-brown; soft, somewhat spongy, with loosely defined vertical strips.

Acknowledgments

I wrote an earlier version of this book, minus the chapter on bark ecology, for my master's thesis at Antioch University New England. I am thankful to everyone there who helped me straddle the worlds of writing and natural history. Tom Wessels, the chair of my thesis committee, helped hatch the original idea for this project. Through numerous conversations and walks in the woods with Tom, I gained many insights about bark that are included in this guide. (His book *Reading the Forested Landscape* was also an important resource.) Without Tom's guidance and encouragement, which has continued since my graduation from Antioch, this book would not have been possible. Critical editing as my deadline drew close, and encouragement all along the way, came from Paul Hertneky. The opportunity to teach bark identification, provided by Peter Palmiotto, helped me organize and refine the text, and Jon Atwood helped with range maps.

Helen Whybrow provided editorial guidance and inspiration, first as a member of my thesis committee, and then throughout the years it took to finish the book and bring it to publication. Other friends and family also have supported me, even if they occasionally wondered what was taking so long. Their encouragement, along with the enthusiasm of many new acquaintances who expressed interest in my book-in-progress, inspired me when the scope and the solitary nature of this project seemed insurmountable. Thanks to all of you.

I am grateful to everyone at the University Press of New England for taking on and fully supporting this project. Their commitment to detail and aesthetics refined my manuscript and made it as beautiful as the trees it describes. Thanks also to the readers of this guide. It is with great satisfaction that I imagine you wandering some wooded parcel, getting to know the trees.

Finally, I could not have persevered without endless love and editorial support from my wife, Samantha, and the inspiration of our children, Leo and Luna. The beauty in every detail of nature—my ultimate motivation for writing this book—is reflected by the wonder in my family's eyes.

Suggested Reading

Many sources listed in the bibliography are technical articles or books from which I have gleaned bits of information about bark ecology or bark structure relevant to the tree species here in the Northeast. Writings for a general readership devoted to bark are limited in number, but two books would make fine additions to your library or coffee table. *Bark*, by Ghillean Prance, Anne Prance, and Kjell Sandved, includes high-quality photographs and descriptions of bark structure, function, and ecology for a variety of species that grow worldwide. (This volume may be hard to find—check with your public library or look for a used copy.) Hugues Vaucher's *Tree Bark* also contains a detailed section on bark structure (written by Ladislav Kucera and Livia Bergamin) along with excellent photographs of bark from around the world. This book includes descriptions and illustrations of bark types that inspired my own bark classification system.

A photographic key to bark is included in *The Tree Identification Book* by George Symonds and Stephen Chelminski; *Identifying Trees* by Michael Williams includes a winter key that relies heavily on bark characteristics. For those looking for more information on non-bark characteristics, *Trees of the Northern United States and Canada* by John Laird Farrar uses excellent descriptions, illustrations, and photographs to describe a comprehensive list of features for each species.

My favorite books on the natural history and ecology of trees include *Trees: Their Natural History*, by Peter Thomas, a remarkably thorough but easy to read volume that explains "how trees work, grow, reproduce, and die"; *Reading the Forested Landscape*, by Tom Wessels, a fascinating book that teaches its readers how to recognize the ecological history of a landscape; John Eastman's *The Book of Forest and Thicket* which, among other things, details many associations between plants and other organisms; and *Trees of New England*, by Charles Fergus, which describes the natural history of each tree species in the region and includes details on human interactions and uses.

Bibliography

"Analysis of Tree Bark Shows Global Spread of Insecticides." (1995). *New York Times* 145: C4.

Adams, D. C., and J. F. Jackson. (1995). "Estimating the Allometry of Tree Bark." *American Midland Naturalist* 134(1): 99–106.

Basey, J. M., S. H. Jenkins, and G. C. Miller. (1990). "Food Selection by Beavers in Relation to Inducible Defenses of *Populus tremuloides*." *Oikos* 59: 57–62.

Bier, J. E. (1964). "The Relation of Some Bark Factors to Canker Susceptibility." *Phytopathology* 54: 250–53.

Bier, J. E., and M. H. Rowat. (1962). "The Relation of Bark Moisture to the Development of Canker Diseases Caused by Native, Facultative Parasites." *Canadian Journal of Botany* 40: 61–69.

Blakeslee, A. F., and C. D. Jarvis. (1913). *Trees in Winter: Their Study, Planting, Care and Identification*. New York: MacMillan Co.

Borger, G. A. (1973). "Development and Shedding of Bark." In T. T. Kozlowski, *Physiological Ecology*, 205–33. New York: Academic Press.

Butin, H. (1995). *Tree Diseases and Disorders: Causes, Biology, and Control in Forest and Amenity Trees*. Oxford: Oxford University Press.

Campbell, C. S., F. Hyland, and M. L. F. Campbell. (1975). *Winter Keys to Woody Plants of Maine*. Orono: University of Maine Press.

Clausen, K. E., and R. M. Godman. (1969). "Bark Characteristics Indicate Age and Growth Rate of Yellow Birch." Research Note NC-75. USDA Forest Service, North Central Forest Experiment Station.

Collingwood, G. H., and W. D. Brush. (1974). *Knowing Your Trees*. Washington, D.C.: The American Forestry Association.

Core, E. L., and N. P. Ammons. (1958). *Woody Plants in Winter: A Manual of Common Trees and Shrubs in Winter in the Northeastern United States and Southeastern Canada*. Morgantown: West Virginia University Press.

Cotter, H. V. T., and R. O. Blanchard. (1982). "The Fungal Flora of Bark of *Fagus grandifolia*." *Mycologia* 74(5): 836–43.

Covington, W. W. (1975). "Altitudinal Variation of Chlorophyll Concentration and Reflectances of the Bark of *Populus tremuloides*." *Ecology* 56: 715–20.

DeRosa, E. W. (1983). "Lightning and Trees." *Journal of Aboriculture* 9(2): 51–53.

Eastman, J. (1992). *The Book of Forest and Thicket*. Mechanicsburg, Penn.: Stackpole Books.

Elias, T. S. (1987). *The Complete Trees of North America: Field Guide and Natural History*. New York: Gramercy Publishing Co.

Ennos, R. (2001). *Trees*. Washington D.C.: Smithsonian Institution Press.

Esau, K. (1965). *Plant Anatomy*. New York: John Wiley and Sons.

Fahn, A. (1974). *Plant Anatomy*. Elmsford, N.Y.: Pergamon Press.

Farrar, J. L. (1995). *Trees of the Northern United States and Canada*. Ames: Iowa State Press.

Foote, K. C., and M. Schaedle. (1978). "The Contribution of Aspen Bark Photosynthesis to the Energy Balance of the Stem." *Forest Science* 24(4): 569–73.

"Forest Trees of Maine." (1995). Maine Forest Service, Department of Conservation. 2004.

Franceschi, V. R., P. Krokene, E. Christiansen, et al. (2005). "Anatomical and Chemical Defenses of Conifer Bark against Beetles and Other Pests." *New Phytologist* 167: 353–76.

Freinkel, S. (2007). *American Chestnut: The Life, Death, and Rebirth of a Perfect Tree*. Berkeley: University of California Press.

Gill, M. A. (1995). "Stems and Fires." In B. L. Gartner, *Plant Stems: Physiology and Functional Morphology*, 323–42. San Diego: Academic Press.

Glass, J. C., and K. Granet. (1978). "Bark Chlorophyll in the American Beech (*Fagus grandifolia*) Varies with Bark Aspect." *American Midland Naturalist* 100(2): 510–12.

Gleason, H. A., and A. Cronquist. (1991). *Manual of Vascular Plants of Northeastern United States and Canada*. Bronx: The New York Botanical Garden.

Grimm, W. C. (1983). *The Illustrated Book of Trees*. Mechanicsburg, Penn.: Stackpole Books.

Haberlandt, G. (1914). *Physiological Plant Anatomy*. London: MacMillan and Co.

Hardin, J. W., D. J. Leopold, and F. M. White. (2001). *Harlow and Harrar's Textbook of Dendrology*. New York: McGraw Hill.

Harvey, R. B. (1923). "Cambial Temperatures of Trees in Winter and Their Relation to Sun Scald." *Ecology* 4(3): 261–65.

———. (1923). "Relation of the Color of Bark to the Temperature of the Cambium in Winter." *Ecology* 4(4): 391–94.

Hawes, A., and W. Mattoon. (1982). *Forest Trees of Southern New England*. Middletown: Connecticut Forest and Park Association.

Hengst, G. E., and J. O. Dawson. (1993). "General Technical Report NC 161;

Bark Thermal Properties of Selected Central Hardwood Species." 9th Central Hardwood Forest Conference. Purdue University, West Lafayette, Ind.

Houston, D. R. (2004). "Beech Bark Disease: 1934 to 2004: What's New since Ehrlich?" Beech Bark Disease Symposium, Rep. NE-331. USDA Forest Service, Saranac Lake, N.Y.

Huberman, M. A. (1943). "Sunscald of Eastern White Pine." *Ecology* 24(4): 456–71.

Humphrey, S. R., A. R. Richter, and J. B. Cope. (1977). "Summer Habitat and Ecology of the Endangered Indiana Bat, *Myotis sodalis.*" *Journal of Mammology* 58(3): 334–46.

Huntington, A. O. (1902). *Studies of Trees in Winter: A Description of Deciduous Trees of Northeastern America.* Boston: Knight and Millet.

Ingham, E. R., and A. R. Moldenke. (1995). "Microflora and Microfauna on Stems and Trunks: Diversity, Food Webs, and Effects on Plants." In B. L. Gartner, *Plant Stems: Physiology and Functional Morphology,* 241–56. San Diego: Academic Press.

Jackson, D. W. (1982). "Tree Bark for Winter Identification." *The Conservationist* 36(4).

Jackson, J. F., D. C. Adams, and U. B. Jackson. (1999). "Allometry of Constitutive Defense: A Model and a Comparative Test with Tree Bark and Fire Regime." *The American Naturalist* 153(6): 614–32.

Karels, T. J., and R. Boonstra. (2003). "Reducing Solar Heat Gain During Winter: The Role of White Bark in Northern Deciduous Trees." *Arctic* 56(2): 168–74.

Kaufert, F. (1937). "Factors Influencing the Formation of Periderm in Aspen." *American Journal of Botany* 24(1): 24–30.

Kucera, L. J., and L. Bergamin. (2003). "The Structure, Function and Physical Properties of Bark." In H. Vaucher, *Tree Bark: A Color Guide,* 21–37. Portland, Ore.: Timber Press.

Little, E. L. (1980). *National Audubon Society Field Guide to North American Trees: Eastern Region.* New York: Alfred A. Knopf.

———. (1999). Digital representation of "Atlas of United States Trees." U.S. Geological Survey. 2009.

McPhee, J. (1975). *The Survival of the Bark Canoe.* New York: Farrar, Straus and Giroux.

Mitchell, R. S., and G. C. Tucker. (1997). *Revised Checklist of New York State Plants.* Albany: New York State Museum.

Nanko, H., and W. A. Cote. (1980). *Bark Structure of Hardwoods Grown on Southern Pine Sites.* Syracuse, N.Y.: Syracuse University Press.

Ostrofsky, W. D., and R. O. Blanchard. (1984). "Variation in Bark Characteristics of American Beech." *Canadian Journal of Botany* 62: 1564–66.

Pearson, L. C., and D. B. Lawrence. (1958). "Photosynthesis in Aspen Bark."
American Journal of Botany 45(5): 383–87.

Peattie, D. C. (1966). *A Natural History of Trees of Eastern and Central North
America*. Boston: Houghton Mifflin.

Perry, T. O. (1971). "Winter-Season Photosynthesis and Respiration by Twigs
and Seedlings of Deciduous and Evergreen Trees." *Forest Science* 17(1):
41–43.

Petrides, G. A. (1958). *A Field Guide to Trees and Shrubs: Northeastern and
North-Central United States and Southeastern and South-Central Canada*.
New York: Houghton Mifflin.

Pfanz, H., and G. Aschan. (2000). "The Existence of Bark and Stem Photosynthesis in Woody Plants and Its Significance for the Overall Carbon
Gain. An Eco-Physiological and Ecological Approach." *Progress in Botany*
62: 477–510.

Prance, G. T., A. E. Prance, and K. B. Sandved. (1993). *Bark: The Formation,
Characteristics, and Uses of Bark around the World*. Portland, Ore.: Timber
Press.

Raven, P. H., R. F. Evert, and S. E. Eichhorn. (1992). *Biology of Plants*. New
York: Worth Publishers.

Sajdak, R. L. (1968). "Variation in Bark Characters and Wood Specific Grav-
ity of Sugar Maple." Proceedings of Eight Lake States Forest Improve-
ment Conference, res. paper NC-23. USDA Forest Service, North Central
Experiment Station, St. Paul, Minn.

Schaedle, M., P. Iannaccone, and K. C. Foote. (1968). "Hill Reaction Capac-
ity of Isolated Quaking Aspen Bark Chloroplasts." *Forest Science* 14(2):
222–23.

Scott, L. I. (1950). "The Changing Surface of the Tree." *The Naturalist* (832).

Seiler, J. R., J. A. Peterson, and E. C. Jensen. (2000). *Woody Plants in North
America*. Dubuque, Iowa: Kendall/Hunt Publishing.

Seiler, J. R., J. W. Groninger, and J. A. Peterson. (2003). Forest Biology Textbook. Virginia Tech, Blacksburg, Va. Available online at http://www.
cnr.vt.edu/dendro/forestbiology/syllabus3.htm.

Shain, L. (1995). "Stem Defense against Pathogens." In B. L. Gartner, *Plant
Stems: Physiology and Functional Morphology*, 383–406. San Diego: Academic Press.

Shigo, A. L. (1983). "Tree Defects: A Photo Guide." Gen. Tech. Report NE-82.
USDA Forest Service, Northeast Forest Experimental Station, Broomall,
Penn.

———. (1986). *A New Tree Biology Dictionary.* Durham, N.H.: Shigo and Trees, Associates.

———. (1989). *A New Tree Biology: Facts, Photos, and Philosophies on Trees and Their Problems and Proper Care.* Durham, N.H.: Shigo and Trees, Associates.

Sorrie, B. A., and P. Somers. (1999). *The Vascular Plants of Massachusetts: A County Checklist.* Westborough: Massachusetts Division of Fisheries and Wildlife Natural Heritage and Endangered Species Program.

Spalt, K. W. (1962). "Bark Characteristics and Fire Resistance: A Literature Survey." Occasional Paper 193. USDA Forest Service, Southern Forest Experiment Station. New Orleans, La.

Stickel, P. W. (1941). "On the Relation between Bark Character and Resistance to Fire." Technical Note 39. USDA Forest Service, Northeastern Forest Experiment Station.

Stokes, D. W. (1976). *A Guide to Nature in Winter.* Boston: Little, Brown and Co.

Stokes, D., and L. Stokes. (1986). *Guide to Animal Tracking and Behavior.* Boston: Little, Brown and Co.

Strain, B. R., and P. L. Johnson. (1963). "Corticular Photosynthesis and Growth in *Populus tremuloides.*" *Ecology* 44(3): 581–84.

Symonds, G. W. D., and S. V. Chelminski. (1958). *The Tree Identification Book.* New York: William Morrow and Company.

Tehon, L. R., and W. R. Jacks. (1933). "Smooth Patch, a Bark Lesion of White Oak." *Journal of Forestry* 31(4): 430–33.

Thomas, P. (2000). *Trees: Their Natural History.* Cambridge: Cambridge University Press.

Trelease, W. (1931). *Winter Botany: An Identification Guide to Native Trees and Shrubs.* New York: Dover Publications.

Van Horn, P. J. "The Quaking Aspen." *Wilderness Way* 7(4). Available online at http://www.wwmag.net/aspen.htm.

Vaucher, H. (2003). *Tree Bark: A Color Guide.* Portland, Ore.: Timber Press.

Voigt, G. K. (1960). "Alteration of the Composition of Rainwater by Trees." *American Midland Naturalist* 63(2): 321–26.

Ward, H. M. (1909). *Trees: A Handbook of Forest Botany for the Woodlands and the Laboratory. Volume V: Form and Habitat.* London: Cambridge University Press.

Wessels, T. (1997). *Reading the Forested Landscape: A Natural History of New England.* Woodstock, Vt.: The Countryman Press.

Whitmore, T. C. (1962). "Studies in Systematic Bark Morphology. 1. Bark Morphology in Dipterocarpaceae." *New Phytologist* 61(2): 191–207.

——— . (1962). "Why Do Trees Have Different Sorts of Bark?" *New Scientist* (312): 330–31.

Whitney, K. D., and R. L. Blanton. (2008). "The Tree Bark Ecosystem." Slide show narrative 129. Educational Images, Elmira, N.Y.

Wood, F. A., and D. W. French. (1965). "Microorganisms Associated with *Hypoxylon pruinatum*." *Mycologia* 57(5): 766–75.

Zavitz, E. J. (1959). *Hardwood Trees of Ontario with Bark Characteristics.* Ontario Ministry of Natural Resources.

Zimmerman, M. H., and C. L. Brown. (1971). *Trees: Structure and Function.* New York: Springer-Verlag.

Index

Numbers in **boldface** refer to the main reference pages for each species in Chapter 6, which include detailed descriptions, illustrations, and photographs.

Numbers in *italics* refer to illustrative material outside of Chapter 6.

Species are listed by their scientific name, primary common name, and secondary common name. Complete information is listed under the primary common name. Entries for scientific names and secondary common names list only the main reference pages for a species; cross-references will then guide the reader to the complete listing.

Abies balsamea, **180–81** (*see also* fir, balsam)
acacia, false, **126–27**
Acer
  negundo, **88–89**
  nigrum, **104–105**
  pensylvanicum, **90–91**
  platanoides, **92–93**
  rubrum, **94–97** (*see also* maple, red)
  saccharinum, **98–99** (*see also* maple, silver)
  saccharum, **100–103** (*see also* maple, sugar)
active periderm, *8*, *11–12*
algae, 86
Amelanchier arborea, **212–13**
American basswood, **236–37** (*see also* basswood, American)
American beech, **128–31** (*see also* beech, American)
American chestnut, 77–78
American elm, **240–42** (*see also* elm, American)
American hornbeam, **116–17** (*see also* hornbeam, American)

American mountain ash, **218–19** (*see also* mountain ash, American)
annual cankers, 77, *77*, 80
arborvitae, eastern, **124–25** (*see also* cedar, northern white)
ash
  American mountain, **218–19** (*see also* mountain ash, American)
  basket, **176–77**
  black, **176–77**
  green, **178–79**
  hoop, **176–77**
  red, **178–79**
  showy mountain, **220–21**
  swamp, **176–77**, **178–79**
  water, **176–77**, **178–79**
  white, **174–75**
    basal scar, *64*
    intersecting ridges, *33*
aspen
  bigtooth, **226–29**
  lenticels, *23*
  golden, **230–33** (*see also* aspen, quaking)
  quaking, **23–33**
    bark photosynthesis, 63
    defense against fungi, 79, *81*
    powdery bloom, 18, 62, 66, 68, 84
    root sprouts, 66
    trembling, **230–33** (*see also* aspen, quaking)
Atlantic white cedar, **120–21**

bacteria, 10, 75, 84
balm of Gilead, **222–23**
balsam, Canadian, **180–81** (*see also* fir, balsam)
balsam fir, **180–81** (*see also* fir, balsam)
balsam poplar, **222–23**
bark
  associations with other species, 82–86
  definition, 7

human use, 71, 75–76, 86
  inner, *8, 12, 13, 14*
  outer, *8, 14, 14*, 18
  phases, 2–3, 15, 37
  photosynthesis, 61–63, 66, 83, 86
  reflective, 66, 68
  thickness, 14, 63–64, 66, 69
bark types
  furrows and ridges, 32–35, 63
  peeling horizontally in curly strips,
    20–21, 62
  scales, plates, and vertical strips,
    26–31, 63
  smooth, unbroken, 10, 18–19
  vertical cracks or seams, 24–25
  visible lenticels, 22–23
basal scar, 64, *64*
basswood, American, **236–37**
  yellow-bellied sapsucker holes, 70
bats, 84
beaver, 71–72, *73*, 226, 230
beech, American, **128–31**
  annual cankers, 77
  bark photosynthesis, 63
  beech bark disease, 77, 80–82, *82*
  black bears, 72
  characteristics and age, 15
  cork skin, *62*
  epiphytes, 83–84
  fire, 64
  fungi, 84
  lightning, 68
  penetration of bark, 69
  porcupines, 71
  reflective bark, 66
  shedding, 84
  slugs, 86, *86*
  smooth, unbroken bark, 10, *11, 19*, 61
  stemflow enrichment, 85
  thickness, 14, 62
  white-tailed deer scrape, *74*
  wrinkles, *69*
beech bark disease, 77, 80–82, *82, 129*
beech, blue, **116–17** (*see also* hornbeam, American)
Betula
  alleghaniensis, **106–107** (*see also*
    birch, yellow)
  lenta, **108–109** (*see also* birch, black)
  nigra, **110–11** (*see also* birch, river)

papyrifera, **112–13** (*see also* birch,
  paper)
papyrifera var. *cordifolia, 113*
populifolia, **114–15** (*see also* birch,
  gray)
betulin, 68, 76, 112
bigtooth aspen, **226–29** (*see also*
  aspen, bigtooth)
birch
  black, **108–109**
    perennial canker, 77
    plates, *29*
  canoe, **112–13** (*see also* birch, paper)
  cherry, **108–109** (*see also* birch,
    black)
  gray, **114–15**
    chevrons, 79–80, *81*
    powdery bloom, 18
  heart-leaved paper, *113*
  paper, **112–13**
    bark in nests, 84
    bark photosynthesis, 63
    betulin, 68, 76
    chevrons, 80
    lenticels, *23*
    multiple bark types, 15, *16*
    peeling horizontally in curly
      strips, 62, 84
    seed production, 66
  red, **110–11** (*see also* birch, river)
  river, **110–11**
    peeling horizontally in curly
      strips, 21
  silver, **106–107** (*see also* birch,
    yellow)
  sweet, **108–109** (*see also* birch,
    black)
  white, **112–13, 114–15** (*see also* birch,
    gray; birch, paper)
  wire, **114–15** (*see also* birch, gray)
  yellow, **106–107**
    frost rib, *67*
    peeling horizontally in curly
      strips, 21
    thickness, 62
bitternut hickory, **156–57**
black ash, **176–77**
black bears, 72, 74, 194
black birch, **108–109** (*see also* birch,
  black)

black cherry, **216–17** (*see also* cherry, black)
black gum, **172–73** (*see also* gum, black)
black locust, **126–27**
black maple, **104–105**
black oak, **154–55** (*see also* oak, black)
black spruce, **188–89**
black walnut, **166–67** (*see also* walnut, black)
blister rust, 78, 194
box elder, **88–89**
branch and leaf pattern, 5, *5*
bur oak, **138–39**
burls, 78, *79*
butternut, **164–65**
juglone, 76
buttonwood, **208–211** (*see also* sycamore)
callous tissue, 78, *79*
cankers
annual, 77, *77*, 80
beech bark disease, 80–82, *82*
blister rust, 78
butternut, 164
chestnut, American, 77–78
perennial, 77, *77*, 78–79, 81–82
target, 79, *80*
Cape Cod, 65
carpenter ants, 70, 81
Carpinus caroliniana, **116–17** (*see also* hornbeam, American)
Carya
cordiformis, **156–57**
glabra, **158–59** (*see also* hickory, pignut)
ovata, **160–61** (*see also* hickory, shagbark)
tomentosa, **162–63**
Castanea dentata, 77–78
cedar
Atlantic white, **120–21**
eastern red, **122–23**
eastern white, **124–25** (*see also* cedar, northern white)
northern white, **124–25**
bark in nests, 84
vertical strips, 30, *31*
vitamin-C, 76
swamp, **120–21, 124–25** (*see also* cedar, northern white)

Celtis occidentalis, **238–39**
Chamaecyparis thyoides, **120–21**
chemical defense, 72, 75–76
cherry
bird, **214–15**
black, **216–17**
burl, *79*
gum, 75
scales, 27
fire, **214–15**
pin, **214–15**
rum, **216–17** (*see also* cherry, black)
chestnut, American, 77–78
chestnut bark beetle, 78
chestnut oak, **142–43**
chevrons, 79–80, *81*, 114–15, *115*
chinquapin oak, **140–41**
cork, *8*, 9–10, 12, 14, 18, 20
cork cambium, *8*, 9–10, 12
cork skin, *8*, 9, 12,
bark photosynthesis, 61–63
cottontail, 71
cottonwood
eastern, **224–25**
ridges broken horizontally, *34*
southern, **224–25** (*see also* cottonwood, eastern)

dogberry, **218–19, 220–21** (*see also* mountain ash, American)
downy serviceberry, **212–13**
Dutch elm disease, 70, 240, 244

eastern cottonwood, **224–25** (*see also* cottonwood, eastern)
eastern hemlock, **204–207** (*see also* hemlock, eastern)
eastern red cedar, **122–23**
eastern white pine, **200–203** (*see also* pine, eastern white)
elm
American, **240–42**
Dutch elm disease, 70
moose, **244–45** (*see also* elm, slippery)
red, **244–45** (*see also* elm, slippery)
slippery, **244–45**
flour from bark, 71
soft, **240–42, 244–45** (*see also* elm, American; elm, slippery)

white, **240–42** (*see also* elm,
American)
elm bark beetle, 70
epicormic buds, 65
epiphytes, 83–84, *84*

Fagus grandifolia, **128–31** (*see also*
beech, American)
fiber, 9, 14, 28, 32, 34–35
fir, balsam, **180–81**
fire resistance, 63
frost crack, 67
resin, 75
fire, 64–66
fire cycle, 65
Fraxinus
americana, **174–75** (*see also* ash,
white)
nigra, **176–77**
pennsylvanica, **178–79**
freezing, 65–66
frost cracks, 65–66, *67*
frost ribs, 66, *67*
fungi (*see also* cankers)
abundance, 84
beech bark disease, 80–82
beneficial, 84
defense against, 10, 76, 79–80, *81*
Dutch elm disease, 70
feeding on sap, 70
hydration, 84
smooth patch disease, 84
furrows and ridges, 32, *32*, 63 (*see also*
ridges and furrows)

gall, 78, *79*
girdled trunk, 71, 77–78
gray birch, **114–15** (*see also* birch,
gray)
green ash, **178–79**
gum, 75, 238
gum
black, **172–73**
weathering, 66, *68*
sour, **172–73** (*see also* gum, black)

hackberry, **238–39**
hackmatack, **182–83**
heart-leaved paper birch, *113*

hemlock
Canada, **204–207** (*see also* hemlock,
eastern)
eastern, **204–207**
beavers, 70–71
fire resistance, 63
flour from bark, 71
stemflow enrichment, 85
tannins, 76
white-tailed deer, 71
wound cork, 78, *79*
yellow-bellied sapsucker holes,
70, *71*
hemlock spruce, **204–207** (*see also*
hemlock, eastern)
hickory, 24
bitternut, **156–57**
mockernut, **162–63**
pignut, **158–59**
vertical cracks or seams, *25*
red, **158–59** (*see also* hickory,
pignut)
scalybark, **160–61** (*see also* hickory,
shagbark)
shagbark, **160–61**
bats, 84
characteristics and age, 11, *12*
shellbark, **160–61** (*see also* hickory,
shagbark)
smoothbark, **158–59** (*see also*
hickory, pignut)
swamp, **156–57**
upland, **160–61** (*see also* hickory,
shagbark)
white, **162–63**
white-heart, **162–63**
hornbeam, American, **116–17**
smooth, unbroken bark, *19*
hophornbeam, **118–119**
human use of bark, 71, 75–76, 86
hummingbird, ruby-throated,
70

infection, 69–82
secondary, 69–70, 81
infestation, 69–82
secondary, 69–70
initial periderm, *8*, 10–12, 18, *20*
inner bark, *8*, 12, 13, *14*

insects, 70, 75–76, 78, 81
  beech scale, 80
  beneficial, 86
ironwood, **116–17**, **118–19** (*see also* hornbeam, American)

jack pine, **192–93**
Juglans
  cinerea, **164–65** (*see also* butternut)
  nigra, **166–67** (*see also* walnut, black)
juglone, 76, 164, 166
juneberry, **212–13**
juniper, red, **122–23**

larch, eastern, **182–83**
largetooth aspen, **226–29** (*see also* aspen, bigtooth)
Larix laricina, **182–83**
lenticels, *8, 12, 13, 22, 22, 23*
  bark photosynthesis, 62
  shedding bark, 83–84
  vertical cracks, 24
lightning, 68
linden, American, **236–37** (*see also* basswood, American)
Liriodendron tulipifera, **170–71** (*see also* tulip tree)
locust, black, **126–27**

maple
  ash leaf, **88–89**
  black, **104–105**
  hard, **100–103** (*see also* maple, sugar)
  Norway, **92–93**
  red, **94–97**
    beaver activity, *73*
    moose scrapes, 72
    shedding, 84
    target canker, 79, *79*
    vertical strips, *31*
    white-tailed deer scrapes, *74*
  river, **98–99** (*see also* maple, silver)
  rock, **100–103** (*see also* maple, sugar)
  silver, **98–99**
    vertical cracks, 11, *12, 17*

soft, **94–97**, **98–99** (*see also* maple, red; maple, silver)
striped, **90–91**
sugar, **100–103**
  fungi, 84
  red squirrel bite marks, 70
swamp, **94–97** (*see also* maple, red)
white, **98–99** (*see also* maple, silver)

mice, 71
mockernut hickory, **162–63**
moose, 72
moosewood, **90–91**
mountain ash
  American, **218–19**
  moose, 72
  showy, **220–21**
musclewood, **116–17** (*see also* hornbeam, American)

nettletree, **238–39**
northern red oak, **150–53**
northern white cedar, **124–25** (*see also* cedar, northern white)
Norway maple, **92–93**
Norway spruce, **184–85**
Nyssa sylvatica, **172–73** (*see also* gum, black)

oak
  black, **154–55**
    fire cycles, 65
    ridges broken horizontally, *34*
  blue, **138–39**
  bur, **138–39**
  chestnut, **142–43**
  chinquapin, **140–41**
  gray, **150–53** (*see also* oak, northern red)
  mossycup, **138–39**
  northern red, **150–53**
    bark phases, *16, 61*
    epiphytes, 83, *83*
    fire tolerance, 64
    lenticels, *13*
    lightning strikes, 68
    penetration, 69
    uninterrupted ridges, *35*

pin, **148–49**
 lenticels, 23
 post, **144–45**
 quercitron, **154–55** (*see also* oak,
  black)
 red, **150–53** (*see also* oak, northern
  red)
 rock, **140–41, 142–43**
 scarlet, **146–47** (*see also* scarlet oak)
 Spanish, **148–49** (*see also* oak, pin)
 stave, **132–35** (*see also* oak, white)
 swamp, **136–37, 148–49** (*see also*
  oak, pin)
 swamp white, **136–37**
 white, **132–35**
 smooth patch disease, 84, *85*
 yellow, **140–41, 154–55** (*see also* oak,
  black)
oilnut, **164–65** (*see also* butternut)
Ostrya virginiana, **118–19**
outer bark, *8*, 14, *14*, 18

paper birch, **112–13** (*see also* birch,
  paper)
peeling horizontally in curly strips,
  20, *20, 21*
perennial cankers, 77, *77*, 78–79, 81–82
periderm, *8*, 9–14
 active, *8*, 11–12
 furrows and ridges, 32
 initial, *8*, 10–12, 18, 20
 peeling horizontally in curly
  strips, 20
 plates, 26, 28
 scales, 26
 smooth, unbroken, 18
 vertical strips, 26, 30
phloem
 active, 8, 9, 12
 exposed in cracks, 24
 in rhytidome, 11–12, 26
photosynthesis
 active phloem, 9
 bark, 61–63, 66, 83, 86
Picea
 abies, **184–85**
 glauca, **186–87**
 mariana, **188–89**
 rubens, **190–91** (*See also* spruce,
  red)

pignut hickory, **158–59** (*see also*
  hickory, pignut)
pileated woodpecker, 70, 81
pin cherry, **214–15**
pine
 eastern white, **200–203**
 beavers, 71–72
 blister rust, 78
 flour from bark, 71
 resin, 75
 gray, **192–93**
 hard, **196–99** (*see also* pine, pitch)
 jack, **192–93**
 northern white, **200–203** (*see also*
  pine, eastern white)
 Norway, **194–95** (*see also* pine, red)
 pitch, **196–99**
 fire resistance, 65
 red, **194–95**
 stemflow enrichment, 85
 scrub, **192–93**
 white, **200–203** (*see also* pine, eastern white)
 yellow, **196–99** (*see also* pine, pitch)
pin oak, **148–49** (*see also* oak, pin)
Pinus
 banksiana, **192–93**
 resinosa, **194–95** (*see also* pine, red)
 rigida, **196–99** (*see also* pine, pitch)
 strobus, **200–203** (*see also* pine,
  eastern white)
pitch pine, **196–99** (*see also* pine, pitch)
planetree, American, **208–211** (*see also*
  sycamore)
Platanus occidentalis, **208–211** (*see also*
  sycamore)
plates, 28, *28, 29*
poplar, **226–29, 230–33** (*see also* aspen,
  bigtooth; aspen, quaking)
poplar, balsam, **222–23**
poplar, Carolina, **224–25** (*see also* cottonwood, eastern)
poplar, tulip, **170–71** (*see also* tulip
  tree)
poplar, yellow, **170–71** (*see also* tulip
  tree)
Populus
 balsamifera, **222–23**
 deltoides, **224–25** (*see also* cottonwood, eastern)